FINDING HOPE WHEN STORMS DON'T CEASE

FINDING HOPE WHEN STORMS DON'T CEASE

An Inspiring True Story of Extraordinary Faith Through the Unimaginable

VALERIE JUILLERAT

DAVID M. RIGDON & AUSTIN V. RIGDON

ISBN: 979-8-9914458-0-1 (Paperback)
ISBN: 979-8-9914458-1-8 (Hardback)
ISBN: 979-8-914458-2-5 (Ebook)

In Loving Memory
Of

B. "Bucky" Walker
June 20, 1942 – July 18, 2022
&
Katelynn Jo Maynus
March 12, 2002 – June 20, 2020

CONTENTS

FOREWORD

By Lance Clark

When I first met Valerie, it was during a routine visit to our tax preparer. She was running a printing business in the same office building, and in just a few moments of conversation, I sensed that I had encountered someone truly remarkable—a woman of unshakable determination and unwavering faith in Christ.

It was clear that Valerie was not just a businesswoman, but someone whose life was grounded in purpose, a purpose she found in her deep and sincere relationship with God. As our conversation continued, I shared with her my dream of producing our first feature film, *A Carpenter's Prayer*, a personal story based on my own childhood encounter with a broken man—a carpenter struggling with addiction and faith, desperately in need of a second chance. Valerie's eyes lit up, and she responded, "I have a story to share with you that you need to hear."

That story, as I would later learn, was far more than I could have imagined. My wife and I sat down with Valerie over breakfast, where she opened her heart to us. She shared the painful, heart-wrenching journey of a mother fighting for her two teenage sons who had been swept into the destructive grip of addiction and rebellion. As Valerie told us about the years of suffering, the anguish of spousal abuse, and the torment of demonic oppression, it became clear that her story was one of not just survival, but of extraordinary faith and triumph through Christ.

Valerie's transparency and courage to share the most vulnerable parts of her life are what make this book so powerful. *Finding Hope When Storms Don't Cease* is more than just a personal testimony—it is a beacon of hope for anyone facing addiction, abuse, or overwhelming trials.

Valerie's unwavering belief that God has a purpose for every trial shines through each page. Her story reveals a mother's relentless love for her sons and a woman's refusal to give up, even in the darkest of times. If you or someone you love is battling addiction, abuse, or spiritual oppression, this book will offer not only comfort but hope—hope that, no matter the storm, God's hand is always at work, and His love knows no bounds.

Valerie's journey will challenge you to see God's power in the waiting, His grace in the trials, and His faithfulness in the deliverance. One of the most profound lessons you will learn in these pages is how prayer becomes a lifeline—a direct connection to the God who hears, heals, and redeems. Valerie shows us that "we must pray with a willingness to wait and wait with a willingness to pray." Her words echo with the truth that God never leaves us to suffer in vain. He uses every storm to shape us, strengthen us, and guide us to the freedom only He can offer. This book is a testament to the power of faith, perseverance, and God's unfailing love. It will resonate with anyone who has ever felt hopeless, lost, or unworthy of God's grace. Through Valerie's story, you will see that no matter how fierce the storm, there is always hope—hope that can only be found in Christ.

Lance Clark, PhD.,
Dean of the Arts, Huntington University
Producer/Director, Forester Film, LLC
Producer of the feature film, *A Carpenter's Prayer*

Praise for Finding Hope When Storms Don't Cease

"I watched Valerie's story in a video for the first time and was as delighted as I was startled-stuck in my seat by the episodes that unfolded in the sequel. I concluded that the story must be told in all formats—literary and audiovisual, and circulated worldwide. Thus, I couldn't be more excited to see that become real in this fine and classic publication.

Storms are a general human experience; everyone has his or her version of stories of 'storms' to tell. Albeit the narratives, the depth of inspiration, the highly valid and indisputable lessons, and the uniqueness of Valerie's story make all the difference—significantly.

I pray that *"Finding Hope When Storms Don't Cease"* will captivate and greatly inspire you as well as it did me."

Bishop Louis Christian Godson (Ph.D.).
Best-selling Author and Executive Leadership Coach
www.LouisChristianGodson.com

"Heart-wrenching. Honest. Captivating. Faith-building. *Finding Hope When Storms Don't Cease* is a page-turner that will touch your heart and propel you to ask God important, soul-searching questions. Valerie Juillerat writes with vulnerability, openness, and a resilient faith that will cause readers to realize they can make it through impossible situations, recurring challenges, and deep disappointments. Read it first for yourself and then make it your go-to gift for people who are dealing with hard circumstances."

Carol Kent,
Founder & Executive Director of Speak Up Ministries
Speaker & Author of *When I Lay My Isaac Down* (NavPress)

To My sons, Austin and David:
Thank you for your courage and willingness
to be transparent with our story in the effort to help others.
You both have amazing hearts,
and I am so proud of you and the men you have become.

To My Loving Husband, Tim:
Thank you for your incredible support and encouragement.
You pushed me when I wanted to quit,
you held my hand when I cried through tough memories,
and you provided for every need during
this whole crazy process.
Thank you!

CHAPTER ONE

The Storm

A black mass of clouds rolled and roiled overhead.

Was a storm coming our way? The intimidating thunderhead swirled and rotated, and there was an anxiety growing in me that I couldn't explain.

The darkness deepened. Threatened. What was this really? A winter storm brewing or something much more powerful and dangerous. Something evil.

I couldn't tear my eyes away as the form expanded, swirled, and drew near. The fear in me was growing as I continued to watch the darkness approaching. I could feel a dark presence as it swooped toward me- coming straight for me as though it could see me. Picking up speed, it rushed forward. I held my breath in fear as it dropped lower. Closer.

Like the voice that taunted me when I was a teenager pushing through the narrow black tunnels of a haunted house, I heard the haughty laugh.

"Hahahaha. I'm coming after you."

Inches from touching me, I squeezed my eyes tightly closed, quickly turned my head away while feeling its breath on my cheek. I tried to pull away but could not move, dreading its touch on my skin. As the frightening presence reached for me, I screamed a cry for help with the only word I could get out.

"Jesus!"

I awoke, sitting straight up in bed. Confused, I blinked against the darkness of my bedroom, finally focusing on the night-light glowing from behind the bathroom door that stood ajar. In the faint light, I recognized the familiar quilted bedspread, maroon and embroidered with black felt flowers.

"Are you okay?" My mom's voice came from the other side of the bed.

I remembered that she had come to visit my two boys and me for a couple of weeks during the Christmas holiday.

"Sorry I woke you." I brushed hair from my forehead, damp with nightmare sweat. "I had a bad dream."

Turning away from her, I pulled the blankets tightly around me and drew my legs into a fetal position.

Mom mumbled something comforting and turned to the other side of the king-size mattress.

Pressing my cheek into the coolness of the soft pillow, I waited for the pounding of my racing heartbeat to slow. But sleep would not come. I'd had nightmares before, but I had never felt such a near presence of evil. So real, so intense, so close to me.

Later, I would come to know this as only the first of a string of dreams leading to a turn of events that would change my life forever. Initially, I thought demons were warning me they were coming after me because God had placed a calling on my life to be a writer and speaker to share my story and give others hope. I soon realized some were demons, but others were God using the dreams to prepare my heart for the raging storms to come.

This particular dream was just the beginning. There were lessons to be learned through the darkness that would penetrate my life for the next three years. Important lessons. Lessons that not only touched my life, but the lives of my two sons.

CHAPTER TWO

Tropical Depression

Τ he door to the small dark entryway leading off the garage opened, and my two sons burst into the kitchen.

Both boys had dark blonde hair and beautiful blue eyes. Both possessed hearts of compassion and generosity. Austin at sixteen was quiet, calculative, and rather shy around people. Austin lit up the room when he smiled. One glance at his contagious grin and I couldn't help but smile, too.

Fourteen at the time, David was adventurous, inquisitive, and extremely creative. David also made me smile, especially through his humor and quick wit. No challenge was too big for him, and he feared nothing—well, almost nothing.

The boy's stepfather and I had met through work. The business was our common point and we loved to dream about new strategies and ways to grow his company. There were hockey games, nights out with the families and then there was his love for the Lord. His level of faith and leadership drew me in. I wanted that in my life. A man who was a spiritual leader.

Leadership took on a whole new meaning over time and so did faith. After nine years of marriage, I had been brought to a place of no longer knowing who *I* was. Although I was emotionally, mentally, and physically drained from my second husband's hurtful words and controlling demeanor, I stayed with him still.

I had already been divorced from the boy's father, and the guilt of being a divorced Christian weighed on me. The thought of people's criticism and judgement all over again, led me to keep us in a bad place way past what others would then classify as unacceptable.

Having spent the weekend with their dad, they carried their overnight duffle bags over one shoulder and slung the straps of their school backpacks over the other. Like most divorced couples with kids, we were on the every other weekend schedule. They made their way across the kitchen, one following the other like ducks in a pond.

Suddenly, as if lying in wait for the sound of their arrival home, their stepdad entered the kitchen from the back room where he spent most of his time alone. I don't recall what he was angry about this time, but the boys froze in the middle of the kitchen under his verbal onslaught.

At six feet tall, he towered over them. His deep intimating voice outlining something he wanted to make sure they knew he didn't like about what they had or had not done.

This scene was common; too common, and to the extent that the relationship between the boys and their stepfather had rapidly dissolved. The tension began to escalate to what could be dangerous levels.

He finished issuing his orders and disappeared back into his man cave. As he turned away, I recognized from the expression on his face that he was pleased he had gained the victory by holding tight to his control over them again.

My teens glanced at me where I sat on the living room couch. Pages of the company bookwork lay in my lap, and the muffled sound of the television show I had been watching played in the background. But in real life, I watched this rerun of a depressing movie that seemed to be on repeat.

There was that look again. All too frequently, their faces held a bewildered expression as they met my eyes and quickly glanced away. Dropping their heads, they passed me without a word. My heart ached for them. Greetings of welcome home and how was your weekend never crossed their stepdad's lips as they went to their rooms. Such innocence. This wasn't fair to them.

Peering over the top of the banister, I watched as they silently climbed the stairs, David following Austin. In the hall light that shone down on them, I saw the silent expression of rage boiling from deep within their souls. Jaws tight, teeth clenched. The joy that had shone in their beautiful blue eyes when they had come home had been replaced with hatred.

It was time. I'd have to live with the physical and emotional effects of our marriage for the rest of my life. After all that we had been put through, I had to protect them from anything more damaging. Even if it was too late to protect myself.

One day, I was confiding in my dear friend Kathy about what we were going through. Kathy was a mature Christian with whom I had developed a beautiful friendship over the course of twenty years. She had become a spiritual mentor, walking beside me through business ventures, personal challenges, and the development of my faith. She was the one I turned to for prayer, advice, and a motherly kind of love. Though living fifty miles apart made it difficult to spend a lot of time together, without judgment she guided, loved, and prayed for me.

Kathy had lived with an abusive alcoholic for many years herself, so I knew she could relate and prayed she could give me guidance. She had remarried and now had a loving Christian man for a husband. Within our conversation, I mentioned that I still loved my husband, despite his cruelty.

"You can say that you love him?" Kathy asked with disbelief in her tone. "Do you mean that?"

"Yes, I do," I assured her.

"How is that possible?"

"I don't know," I said. "But I do."

Kathy considered her own experience. "I couldn't after everything he put my children through."

Kathy's bitter tone was uncharacteristic of her. I was shocked at her words. At the same time, I understood. She would get no judgment from me. I had been there.

The truth is, I couldn't explain my love for my husband. No one else except his family seemed to be able to understand my feelings either. There was just something about that man that brought me to love him at a very deep level that didn't and wouldn't go away despite the continuing turmoil.

Earlier, the boys and I lived in our home with a big backyard in a pleasant subdivision. The houses were spaced adequately apart but close enough to encourage residents to be neighborly.

Bob, my first husband and the father of Austin and David, and I had bought the house together. As a youngster, Austin had a special friend he liked to spend time with who lived down the street, Rachel. Rachel was tall and slender with long brunette hair. In our quiet neighborhood, the boys made friends with the kids who lived nearby.

That year, we hosted a birthday party for Austin with extended family as guests. We set up white folding chairs in our garage and decorated tables with streamers and balloons. A food table with all the trimmings was positioned crosswise in front of the other tables for easy access to the wide array of party food. Austin's special guest was Rachel.

When the meal was finished, I placed a folding chair center stage from the tables, so the party guests could watch as he opened each gift. Wrapped in pretty pink paper, the first package was from his Uncle Steve. Austin smirked knowingly as he carefully tore away the paper. His giggling escalated into rolling laughter causing his face to turn red and the veins to pop out on his neck. Others laughed at how hard the birthday boy was laughing.

Inside the carefully wrapped package was a Barbie doll. His uncle was known for teasing, and Austin got it.

To our surprise, Austin got up from his chair, made his way across the garage in front of all his guests, and sweetly gave the Barbie doll to Rachel. That gesture and Austin's birthday were moments I remembered in our much loved home.

Unfortunately, I couldn't afford to stay there after their father and I divorced. Instead, a black and gold For Sale sign was posted in the front yard. The house I enjoyed with a gas fireplace, large master bath, walk-in closet, and vaulted ceilings was small enough to be manageable and affordable for our family. Until I couldn't afford it anymore on a single mom's income.

The home sold quickly, and the following month I searched for a new place for me and my sons to live. Giving up our home was difficult enough, but what made things worse was the cash buyers were a couple who both had plans to *unexpectedly* leave their spouses and hook up with this as their new residence.

Normally, a cash purchase is an advantage, but not in my case this time. Instead of the usual thirty days, while the banks get the paperwork together and appraisals are completed, the buyers wanted to take possession in two weeks. Working full time, while single and with two children to pack and move, I was uncertain where we would move to.

Austin struggled with moving away from his best friend.

"This is all your fault," Austin accused one day when we talked about him not being able to see Rachel as was his normal routine.

He was right. It was my fault, and my heart broke for him. I never thought Bob and I would divorce. We had been together for nineteen years. It took me five years just to decide to marry him. And now our children suffered because of our decisions.

CHAPTER THREE

Tropical Disturbance

We had just moved into his house, my next relationship, the weekend before.

Friday evening, he watched sports as he always did when he came home from work. I was busy unloading and organizing the many boxes I still needed to unpack from the move.

The house was a manufactured home with an open concept, and I was in the kitchen diligently unpacking my belongings. In the cabinets filled with his pots and pans, I fitted kitchenware into where I found space. I had already put away the wide assortment of plastic bowls and lids with no real rhyme or reason. Mixing, matching, and stacking the plasticware with bowls of so many colors, shapes, and sizes wasn't fitting very well in the allotted space.

I reached above my head to put plates away in the oak cabinet over the small countertop when I was startled by his angry voice.

"Get over here and clean up this mess!" He had been drinking his usual Friday night favorite, Captain Morgan and Coke. "That is just fricken' ridiculous. You're not going to keep my kitchen cabinets looking like that. You get over here and clean that s$%t up!"

This was the first time I had seen him behave like this. Not knowing what he would do next, I quickly and quietly walked to the cabinet where he stood, hands on hips, staring me down like a parent angry with their child.

I sat on the cold linoleum floor in my pjs, crossed my legs, and rearranged the tupperware and plastic bowls on the lower two shelves in neatly positioned rows and stacks the best I could manage. He walked to the kitchen counter and poured glass number six of the Captain.

All the while, my heart raced, and I silently prayed, "God, help me meet his expectations and let there be no further outbursts or ramifications."

This wouldn't be the last night the cork would blow.

It was difficult to have a normal family life. My husband's mood swings made it hard to find a balance and know what would be right one day and what would suddenly become wrong the next.

If the evening meal I prepared wasn't what he wanted, he yelled, "I'm not eating that s$%t! I'll get my own supper."

I always fixed enough food for supper for the four of us. I felt it was important for the children to eat together at the dining room table; that was family time. A time to pray together, learn about their day, and guide them in their struggles. The evening meal was the time of day to bond as a family.

"Are you some kind of freaking hillbilly?" My husband roared in sarcastic laughter. "That's hillbilly food."

I really wasn't certain what constituted hillbilly food, but obviously my choice of menus didn't meet his standard.

The boys and I took our seats around the oakwood dining room table with a hot meal ready and plates set in position. I extended yet another invitation to him. "Supper is ready, are you going to eat with us?"

He sat in his favorite worn out corduroy recliner in a dark corner of the living room. His arm arched back over his head, leg hiked up over the arm of the chair, using his left foot to rock the chair, his eyes glued on his favorite sports channel. "What are you having?"

"Fish sticks, tater tots, baked beans, and pears."

"No, I'm not eating that slop. I'll fix my own."

This repeated night after night until I eventually stopped asking and only made enough for the boys and me. The three of us sat at the supper table as a family, but one chair was always empty.

Eventually, he did his own food shopping, and I was given an allowance for groceries for me and the boys. We weren't allowed to eat any of his food. It was a challenge to divide the refrigerator and try to teach a five- and seven-year-old that they could not have certain foods in the fridge because they weren't ours to eat.

I made sure my husband understood he was always welcome to eat anything purchased for me and the boys. After all, we were a family.

Every Friday and Sunday night, he arrived home from work at 6:00 p.m. and drank until he passed out in the recliner. I counted the shiny blue and silver aluminum cans that he lined up along the kitchen counter. I knew what to expect at each level of consumption.

1. All good
2. Still calm
3. Giddy and happy
4. Relaxed and loopy
5. Mouthy
6. Belligerent
7. Explosive
8. Best disappear and stay out of the way

But even disappearing didn't always work.

This particular Sunday night, after unpacking a few more boxes, I went to bed around 11:00 p.m. as usual. I was still trying to get settled in our new residence. The boys were home from their weekend stay with their dad. Both were sound asleep in their new rooms, tucked away quietly, and snuggled down in their twin beds covered up with plushy Steelers or Cubs blankets. All their Batman toys, Gameboy games, and books were neatly in place.

Five-year-old David was still a little scared of the dark, especially in a new room with new surroundings, and new sounds to adjust to. I turned on the Batman figure night-light that sat next to his bed on the little white nightstand. The blue glow illuminated the room, so David could see there were no monsters.

Or were there?

Suddenly, my bedroom door was flung open. The room was instantly filled with a blinding light. Startled, I sat up, trying to get my bearings while not knowing what had just happened or why.

Sounding like a raging elephant, my husband consumed the doorway with one hand still on the doorknob and one on the light switch. "You get your @$s in there and turn out that night-light. David is no baby. He doesn't need a night-light," he yelled in outrage. "Get out of that bed right now, and go turn it off. There will be no nightlights in this house."

I was still new to seeing this side of him. Not knowing what else his drunken state might cause him to do, I stumbled around the best I could to get out of the king-size bed. My side of the room had only a small gap to walk between the white stucco painted wall and the mattress. My body felt like it was still half asleep, and the blood flow had not fully reached my legs when my feet hit the floor.

I stumbled over to him, my heart pounding so hard I could hear it in my head. He never moved from the doorway. I had to brush past him in order to exit the room. I had never been in an environment like this before. *What should I do? What should I not do? What is he about to do?*

I looked up into his enraged face as he glared down and followed me with his eyes. He had the look of power and control like a Roman soldier ready to whip his prisoner. And I noticed something I had never seen before—his hazel eyes had turned solid black.

CHAPTER FOUR

Unsettling Waves

The night I heard David crying in his room was the night I decided to do what I could to try to protect their little hearts.

It was another Sunday night of drinking. Lately, he had escalated to hard liquor like rum or vodka, so I could no longer count aluminum cans, and he could hide his consumption level. This new development made it a little more challenging to know what stage he was at in the drinking cycle and how to manage the emotions of the night.

He started drinking earlier than normal that evening and became belligerent earlier than usual.

The boys had come home from their dad's earlier on that Sunday evening. Austin and David hadn't been in bed very long.

My husband was sitting in his usual rocker recliner on his side of the room watching his forty-three-inch plasma screen TV, and I was sitting on the other side of the room watching the old fifty-four-inch projection screen TV. The crossing of the sound from the two sets didn't always make it pleasurable to watch television. His sports channel with blaring enthusiastic sportscasters and crowds cheering made it difficult to even hear the crime stories I enjoyed watching.

"Turn it down," he frequently ordered from across the room.

We had struck up a conversation regarding one of my family members who had met us at church that Sunday. The topic started as an innocent and nonchalant conversation, and then something that was said set him off. In five minutes, tensions went south, and he began verbally ripping her apart; calling her names and attacking her character. In my attempt to defend her and negate his perception of her, his voice escalated. Then he turned the tables and directed his furry toward me and what he felt was my weakness and inability to stand up for myself.

I heard the sound of a whimper coming from David's room. The plush oversized recliner I sat in was positioned across from David's open bedroom door. In the light filtering in from the living room, I saw that his little body was under the covers with his head buried in his pillow. I thought maybe he had experienced a bad dream.

I got up from my rocker and went into David's bedroom to console him, and to find out what upset him so much to bring him to tears.

Lovingly, I bent over his bed in the darkness and whispered, "What's wrong, Davie?"

Sniff...sniff..."I don't like it when he's mean to you," he choked through his tears.

I swallowed against the lump that suddenly formed in my own throat. His words of compassion caught me off guard. Even at five years old, David had a soft spot for his momma.

"It's going to be okay, honey." I gently kissed him on the head and smoothed his soft blonde hair. The bad dream I thought he was having was our reality invading his safe space.

From that night on, I had the boy's father keep Austin and David on Sunday evenings to help avoid subjecting them to a man's drunkenness at least one less night of the week. If I could just eliminate the tension altogether, but that was going to be impossible.

Over time, the environment darkened, and I was constantly seeking a way to manage our life. I longed to find as much peace as I possibly could, especially for the boys.

I started watching movies with my husband every Friday evening. I discovered if we didn't turn the movie on until around 9:00 p.m. on the nights I didn't have the kids, I could make an excuse to stay at work until at least 8:00 p.m. I knew if I waited until movie time to arrive home, I could avoid the first rounds of drinking, and then he would be engrossed enough in the movie he wouldn't start verbally attacking me or my family with his vulgar words. Instead he'd lash out at the characters in whatever film we watched. That I could handle because I could detach from it.

I learned to slow my breathing and psychologically let his yelling at the television roll off like I hadn't heard him. Training myself to be desensitized helped me control how much stress my body received. Or so I thought. On nights when I was lucky, he passed out in his chair by the end of the movie, and I slipped away to bed with a fairly uneventful evening.

My body became taxed from the ongoing years of distress from these living conditions, which caused irreversible physical damage to my health. I hadn't realized how silently stress damaged my body until one day I saw I had dropped twenty pounds without trying. My arms showed a rapid loss of muscle mass. The medical test showed the physical damage was already done, but by this time, that wasn't the only consequence of the situation.

Three times I left. Three times I came back, trying everything I knew to do to try to save our marriage. I tried being submissive, obeying, and remaining quiet. Next, I switched to yelling back, attempting to stand my ground. Another technique I tried was avoidance. I went to counseling, tried using love and kindness, and I tried praying a lot. Nothing I did resulted in a change in his behavior.

One night, he sat in his recliner in the family room, and I sat in my recliner in the living room with the open space in between us. We were having a conversation and talking across the two living areas. He got upset over whatever I attempted to explain to him.

In response, he yelled, talked over me, and antagonized me with his words. This was his usual way of controlling the conversation. He behaved as if he couldn't hear another voice in the room. He was the only one with a microphone.

I stood, the TV remote in my hand, as I attempted to get his attention to calm down. Instead, he increased his volume as if by silencing me he remained in control. He continued to go on and on until I suddenly flung the remote furiously into the seat of my recliner. I needed to be able to say something within the conversation. To that point, he had done all the speaking which was the case most of the time.

I thought throwing the remote would get his attention, and it did. Shocked, his mouth dropped open, and his eyes widened as if I had thrown the remote at him. Certainly, I had wanted to, but that wasn't me. For a moment, I had the response I had hoped for, and he stopped yelling long enough for me to speak and bring the chaos down to a more bearable level.

No matter what method I used, our marriage was slipping away to a darker place. I took long walks almost every evening during the warm weather months, partly to stay away from him, but mostly to pray. The beautiful and peaceful countryside overlooked the corn fields and wooded areas. Seldom did a car drive by and interrupt the sound of nature's music as the sound of singing birds surrounded me.

On those evenings, I threw on my tennis shoes, went out the front door of the house, and made my way down the stone driveway to the asphalt road. That moment felt like entering a gate to heaven and leaving the world behind. My own serene space with God. I walked toward the stop sign about a mile down the road feeling light and free. I didn't look back until I was forced by time and light to return home.

One night as I walked, I glanced down and noticed a pretty pale-yellow butterfly with black spots on its wings that had died along the roadside; and then another one, and another. I remembered how I had used the analogy after returning home the last time that he was like a beautiful butterfly emerging from his cocoon, the representation of the transformation into a loving husband. After separating for a while and some counseling, he had become kind and tender. He worked hard to be a good husband. He was loving and patient.

Returning home, the effort would only last about a year, and then he didn't need to try so hard anymore. I was back where he wanted me. His behavior would return to the angry, controlling bully he had been before. The dead butterflies seemed to symbolize my marriage. Our relationship wasn't going to survive; we were dying inside, and what was once a beautiful rendition of my renewed husband now lay motionless on the rocky black pavement.

I talked, I yelled, and I cried out to God to change things. Amidst buckets of tears, I persistently called out, "God, please help us."

CHAPTER FIVE

Cast Overboard

"Get your stuff," he yelled, "and your kids, and get out!"
That was the third time I packed the kids, and we left. At that point, I was exhausted and couldn't go through the overwhelming stress anymore.

During the previous separation, the boys and I lived with my parents in their basement. The second time, I bought the kids and me a cute little white ranch house in a nice quiet neighborhood within walking distance of the school where the boys attended. I repainted and recarpeted and turned the house into our cozy space. Our safe place.

I no longer had a bed because the king-size bed was his, so I bought a set of used bunk beds for the boys and used Austin's army green and black futon for myself. It wasn't the most comfortable mattress to sleep on, and we had to sacrifice some extras, but the ability to relax we gained was invaluable and worth nights on the futon.

Peace had entered our home again, but strangely enough I missed him. There was a different, more fun and loving side of him that existed, that I missed. I was still in love with that version of him.

He and I remained separated for a year. I had filed for divorce, but neither of us could go through with finalizing. I withdrew the paperwork just before the deadline for him to pen his signature.

David had been younger when we married. The two of them had a unique bond. The day I told the boys we were leaving, David's face wilted, and I could see heartbreak across his face. Returning home, was easy for him, but not so much for Austin. His stepdad had scared him one too many times.

I rented my house to a homeless family, and for the third time, I moved back with him to give our relationship one more try. Surely the year of separation and counseling had made us strong enough to make it through just about anything now. With that mindset, we decided to build our dream home on the piece of land we had purchased years before.

Soon, we watched as a bright orange excavator fired up with a roar that echoed across the grassy land. I felt excitement and hope for the future as the machine sank its large teeth into the ground, breaking the top layer of sod. Layer by layer, the machine scooped buckets of dark soil and piled the loose dirt in a huge mound. The hill grew as the hole expanded to become the space where the foundation of our new house would be.

We returned that evening to see what progress had happened on the first day of construction. The boys jumped out of the car and ran to the freshly dug crater. In his red zip-up hoodie, David reached the top of the enormous mound of dirt and stood on the peak.

I pulled my cell phone from my jacket pocket and snapped photos to capture this moment. David looked so small next to the gigantic hole in the ground that was soon to be the basement. Full size and fully decorated with plush carpet, big screen TV, a ping pong table, and walls painted theater red and hung with sports posters and family pictures. When I was growing up, my friends had rooms like this. Finally, my children would have an inviting space where they could hang out on weekends with their friends and make childhood memories.

"Look, Mom, I'm king of the mountain." David perched above the shell that would hold the future memories we would store away in our hearts in the days to come.

In my eyes, David was king, the young version of the scriptural King David whom he was named after, along with our cousin David who was like a brother to me. All David needed was his slingshot and a few stones. He would need these weapons for the giants he would face in the years ahead.

Before long, the rusty iron grid posts were in place, and the smooth gray concrete foundation was poured. The two-by-fours were next, standing erect like toothpicks in their appropriate crisscross frame that formed a maze the boys liked to venture through, poking their heads through empty sections that would soon hold drywall.

By winter, we knew it would be spring before we could move in. The boys and I stopped by the building site on occasion and walked through the empty wood frames, planning each room and dreaming about how to decorate our own individual spaces.

In the cold outdoor temperatures, the mist from our breath looked like clouds as we talked and giggled. Our dream was coming true. A couple of years earlier, the three of us had walked the parcel of land. One weekend, we walked a Jerico march, a big circle around and around seven times where we wanted the house to stand and silently prayed to God to bless us with this house.

Our prayer was answered, and the dream home had come to fruition. In May, our two story, cedar-colored, Cape-Cod home with the two dormer windows and the pretty red door would be move-in ready.

However, the consistent characteristic of my husband was the inconsistency of his behavior. Just as I relaxed and allowed hope and joy for our future to begin to grow, he started distancing himself from me and the boys.

With the house under construction, I held onto the hope that once we were moved in, he'd find happiness on the new land with a fully stocked pond and his new man cave; a special room built just for him off our bedroom where he could have as much solitude away from all of us as he needed. If our marriage didn't survive, I reasoned that at least this time I had a stable home for my children. I wasn't going to be told to "get my kids and get out" like had occurred months before. I had an investment in this property. He had given me the land in our prior separation, and I took over the payments. We already agreed I'd be paying for this house.

The day arrived when we were scheduled to sign the closing documents and receive the keys to our new home. The lady from the building company arrived early and greeted me with a smile as she stood in the brand-new kitchen. The beautiful black granite island sparkled, and the rich red walls and dark walnut cabinets smelled of new paint and wood.

The sweet lady representing the building company and I chatted as we waited for him to arrive. This was the joyous moment I had anticipated for so long. Incidentally, our conversation became awkward as the scheduled time to sign the final paperwork came and passed. There was still no sign of my husband.

"Here is a goodie bag from us." She handed me a red plastic gadget with a white plastic circular blade snapped into the middle. "Just a little something to show our appreciation for being able to do business with you."

"I've never seen a pizza cutter like that. I look forward to trying it out." I glanced out the window, but no car had entered the driveway. "I'm sorry, I'm not sure where he is. He knew the time. This really isn't like him to be late."

"Well," she checked the time on her phone. "I actually only need one signature."

"Oh, really?" I took the red pen she handed me.

"Go ahead and sign here and here." She pointed to each signature line on the form.

"I'm really sorry." I signed the yellow carbon page acknowledging I had received the keys to the house. "He must have gotten delayed at the office."

Nonetheless, inside of me, I began to suspect he had not planned to show up. He liked playing such games, finding ways he could manipulate a person or situation.

"Here's the keys." She handed me two sets. "Congratulations on your new home. It's beautiful."

"Thank you," I spoke as cheerfully as I possible, hiding any signals of the other emotions I felt. Internally, my happiness to have the new dream home conflicted with the awareness that this marriage milestone we were supposed to share was now tainted. He had prevented this from being the picturesque moment married couples typically have when they've just received the keys to their custom-built dream home. This particular moment might have made a difference in my ability to trust he had our best at heart. To prove he wanted a happy home together. A fresh start for us all.

A few minutes later, the door to the garage opened, and he walked into the kitchen. His face held a dark scowl. I could read in his body language that his delay was intentional. He wanted me to worry. He wanted to make me think he wasn't going to show up and sign the papers.

He gave no apologies for being late. Surprise flickered across his expression when he was told that his signature was not needed. The paperwork was complete.

His attempt to control and dampen the situation backfired on him this time, but this incident set the stage for the storm to come.

CHAPTER SIX

The Derecho

The room was ten feet by ten feet and held his forest green rocker recliner. Next to that chair was the old, beige recliner, the corduroy fabric on the legs scratched down to the bare wood by our cat, Dixie.

A small oak lamp stand was positioned between the chairs as a place to set his glass. On the floor in front of the stand lay magazines and newspapers scattered about that he read on occasion. Across from the sitting area was the black entertainment center with the forty-three-inch TV. The room was his space away from everything else. Away from *everyone* else.

Once we moved into the new house and settled, he spent most of his time in *his room*. I only recall one time when he came to the family room in the basement to watch a movie with the boys and me. He came out of the den long enough to heat a microwave dinner or fix himself a sandwich and then disappear again. On an exceptionally rare occasion when he was hungry enough, and the aroma of what I made for supper appealed to him, he would sit at the kitchen table for a meal with us.

On his wish list when we designed the floor plans for the house, he wanted a porch across the full front of our Cape Cod home. Extra wide, the concrete porch had plenty of room for a double-seat swing and a set of wicker chairs so all four of us could sit together in the evenings and on weekends. At our previous home, he often sat outside and looked across the field. Now the view included a pond with a field and woods. The redwing blackbirds sang as they perched picture-perfect on the tips of cattails.

One night, I glanced out the bedroom window and noticed him sitting on the swing by himself. I went outside to sit beside him like we used to do at the old home. In those early good days, we spent hours talking about our workday and making plans for the business. The one thing that initially drew us together was the business. All too soon, I discovered the company was about all we seemed to have in common.

This night was different from the nights when we sat on the swing at our previous address. Everything *now* was different. We shared some small talk, but he didn't seem interested in chatting. I attributed the awkwardness to him being tired, but that would be the last time he sat on the front porch with me. From that day forward, he kept to himself next to his grill on the small concrete patio at the back of the house.

The evenings when he grilled chicken or barbecued were the opportunity for the boys and me to spend quality time with him. Grilling was the only thing he had patience for. He layered chicken with hickory smoke barbeque sauce, waiting for hours next to the grill for the meat to slowly cook. Our ongoing joke had been that he would one day sell his special brand of Rando's BBQ Chicken.

One evening, I joined him on the back patio while he grilled. Again I tried to create small talk, but he sat silent, staring at the thick green foliage of the woods behind the house. With my cell phone, I snapped his photo. He turned his face toward me, but there was no smile. Just a somber man in a white muscle T-shirt. He stared at me with lifeless eyes.

Click. That photo was the last memory of the two of us sitting together. He seemed to desire to sit by himself in silence. From that evening forward, I sat on the front porch, his dream porch, while he preferred his rusty black chair on the back slab.

In these solitary hours, I began to spend a lot of time with another love of my life.

We went on, living with a widening distance in our relationship. One day, I parked our gold SUV in the garage. Dressed in blue polyester soccer jerseys with black socks pulled up to their knees, the boys got out of the car, slung their duffle bags and tied-together soccer shoes over their shoulders as they followed me into the house.

Inside, suddenly he appeared through the bedroom doorway leading into the kitchen.

"David, that is not where your shoes go." One hand pointed in David's face and the other rested on his hip. "Pick up your shoes and stop leaving them lying around. We aren't pigs around here. We don't live in a barn."

My anger flared. We had just walked in the door, had not even had time to set down our things, and it seemed like he never had any mercy for the kids.

"Why don't you back off of him." Weary of his demands and criticism, I surprised myself with what came out of my mouth. "All you ever do is bellow orders all the time at these kids."

His mouth dropped open, and his eyes widened. David quickly snatched up his shoes from where he had left them next to the oak kitchen chair where we sat while taking off our shoes.

Both boys rushed through the living room without a word and climbed the stairs with their bags and soccer shoes still in hand. I heard their footsteps hit the landing, and each quickly closed their bedroom doors behind them.

His tone was furious. "What did you say to me?"

"You are constantly on them about something." I sat my armload of stuff on the kitchen table. "We just walked in the door. You never come out of your room or talk to them unless you want to bark orders. You need to back off!"

"Don't you talk to me that way." He moved to the black granite island, placed his hands on the counter, and leaned toward me. "Or I will make life for you and the boys a living hell."

Oh, God, if this gets worse for them, one of those young boys is going to snap, and then... "And find yourself with a gun to your head."

My instant response was prompted by the images running through my head of a movie where a teenage boy who couldn't take any more of his stepfather's abuse shot him. It was a reaction, and once the words were out, there was no going back.

"Do I need to call the sheriff and tell him what's going on?"

"Go ahead," I challenged. "Because I'm pretty certain he already knows exactly what's going on here."

He looked at me with surprise and a little confusion.

I had no worries if he called the sheriff because I wasn't going to be the one having to answer for the ongoing emotional abuse that had taken place in our home for years, and I personally had a long history of friendship and connections with the sheriff and his deputies.

With his threat so boldly proclaimed, the image replayed in my mind of the night the boys walked up the stairs with a growing rage etched on their faces. I knew it was time. I knew what I had to do for the safety of my young teen boys, my health, and even for my husband's sake. I had to remove us from the harmful effects the relationship had on our lives before something devastating happened, and that tragedy would be one more thing from which there would be no going back.

A few months later, the argument we had that evening when I brought the boys home from soccer came up in conversation. He thought I had insinuated that *I* would shoot him, which was the furthest thing from my mind. The reality was I feared for the emotional and mental state of my boys. I feared for my husband despite our fractured relationship. I still loved him, and thankfully, I was given the opportunity to explain what and who I meant and why it was said.

I knew he loved me, but not enough to change in the ways he needed to for us to survive; not enough to be the husband a man of God is called to be. No man is perfect, or woman for that matter, but there is no room for abuse in a marriage. "Husbands, love your wives, as Christ loved the church and gave himself up for her," says Ephesians 5:25 ESV. God calls the man to love the woman. "Wives, submit to your own husbands, as to the Lord," says Ephesians 5:22. God instructs the woman to respect her husband. In our marriage, it had become difficult to find the action of either one. After eight years of trying, there was little hope we were going to find the change that absolutely had to take place.

I had left a few times for a while to gain back my own sanity. Then we tried again to make our relationship work. Each time he gave the effort his all for about a year. In that renewal season, life for me was great. He could be kind and caring. He was able to sit and listen to my thoughts and ideas, and we dreamed dreams together again. He opened my door, did things that made me feel special, and used words of affirmation like, "Well, there's my beautiful wife."

Eventually though, the efforts wore off, and he went back to his normal demeaning habits. I found myself married, but so very alone. Our normal was not what a normal marriage was supposed to be. At least not how I interpreted what God proclaims marriage should be in Scripture.

Abuse can come in many forms including emotional, financial, mental, physical, and sexual. I didn't believe God expected me to stay in an abusive relationship.

Stepping away from the marriage also meant stepping away from the business I loved. With a degree in marketing and design, I had a passion for growing and structuring businesses. My husband often told me I had an anointing in those areas. The last year we worked the business together as a team, and we reached a half-a-million dollars in sales. The business was profitable. From his perspective, this was the best year the company had ever had. What we had been doing together to succeed in business had worked.

Before we got married, he asked me to sign a prenuptial agreement. A friend of the family who married us, encouraged me not to sign.

"Distrust will only set the stage in your marriage," she counseled.

I didn't take her words lightly, but at the time, I just wanted to marry him. I didn't care about the ownership of his business. That wasn't my purpose for marrying him. We were getting married because I loved him and wanted to share my life with him.

Years later, I came to understand her words of wisdom and realized she was right. Signing the prenuptial agreement meant that when I left, I had to walk away from the nine years of hard work I had invested into growing and strengthening his, not our, printing business.

CHAPTER SEVEN

Sudden Squall

Perched on the end of the examination table, I spoke with the physician about my latest health struggles.

We had done many tests to find out why my energy level was so low. Originally, my husband arranged for me to see his doctor, and the three of us had a strange kind of friend-professional relationship. We could share easily and tease each other.

The doctor studied my bloodwork. "Do the two of you still talk?"

"We do," I replied. "We still care about each other."

"I need him to return my calls." He solemnly met my gaze. "He's an extremely sick man."

I frowned, confused. "What does that mean?"

He shook his head. "Of course, I can't share details, but if you have any relationship left with him, talk to him about coming back in to see me."

I left my appointment in a daze. I got into the car, warm from sitting in the sun, and stared out the window. "God, if you knew he was sick, why would you let the divorce go through?"

Considering the events of recent months and inserting this troubling news, I felt sick to my stomach as I continued to pray. "Why didn't you tell me sooner? I wouldn't have left had I known. Who is going to take care of him?"

Though God didn't answer my question about who would care for him, He told me something else. Due to privacy issues, the doctor couldn't share with me what illness he had, but God did. I drove home knowing the man I still loved but couldn't live with, the man who was no longer my husband but my friend, was very sick indeed.

Recalling his recent behavior, he appeared to have little energy and even less interest in much of anything. A few months before we signed the final divorce papers, I begged him to have bloodwork done to find out what was wrong.

"The doctors will do all kinds of tests and charge me all kinds of money," he said stubbornly. "And they still won't give me any answers."

I recalled when we were first married, and I had experienced chest pain and rapid heartbeat, he stood over me and said, "Don't you dare go to the doctor until you get some insurance." He pointed his finger in my face. "You are not going to bury me in debt with medical bills."

That was the day I realized I had made a mistake when I married this man. But it was too late, the vows had been made, I was in this relationship for the long haul—until I couldn't anymore.

Later, we sat on his front porch and looked out across the bean field. We hadn't shared this view in a long time. As we talked about the kids and the business, I quietly prayed he would open up to me on his own and tell me what was happening with his health.

Finally, I gently whispered, "I know that you have leukemia."

He stared at me in surprise. "Who told you that?"

"God told me." I explained my interaction at the doctor's office. "Your friend did not reveal the details. God did."

He didn't believe me, but that was okay for now. I encouraged him to tell his family. "They need to know," I said.

He refused. He wanted God to heal him and was afraid the fear others felt would counteract his faith. "I don't want prayers spoken out of fear."

I prayed if he went into the hospital, God would allow me to be there and take care of him. I asked God for his family to be agreeable to my help.

A few months later, on a beautiful summer evening, the call came.

I was sitting on the porch with bookwork spread across the glass patio tabletop. The convenience of the laptop allowed me to sit outside and listen to the birds and enjoy the sun while I worked. The boys were with their dad, so it was just me in the peace and quiet of the evening.

My cell phone rang, and I saw Jose's name on the caller ID. He was our lead and only screen printer at that time and my ex-husband's roommate. Typically, Jose phoned with questions about a customer's order. Why would he call after business hours?

When I answered, I could hear something heavy in his voice.

"Hello, Princess. How are you doing?" Princess was a nickname he gave me after I had married his boss.

"I'm doing good, Jose. How are you?"

"Valerie, I don't know what to do. He is really sick. I keep telling his family, and they won't listen. Something is wrong, and I think he needs to go to the hospital. I know you aren't married anymore, but I know you still love each other. Would you come and look at him?"

"Jose," I replied, "I don't think he's going to listen to me."

"Please!" His voice rose an octave. "Something is wrong."

"All right." I wondered if I could be of any help. Then I remembered my prayer, asking God to let me care for him. "I'll be there in a little bit."

Not knowing what the evening ahead would hold, I tossed night clothes, a fresh outfit, and my makeup in my black overnight bag. Whatever happened, I wanted to be prepared for whenever I was needed.

It was already dark and getting late as I got into the car and drove the all too familiar twenty-minute route from my house through the country to his home. Headlights greeted me with each passing vehicle while questions whirled in my mind. What would I walk into? How would he respond when I arrived? Especially this late at night. Would he get angry and belligerent? Would he send me right back home? Would he possibly be surprisingly happy to see me? Would he cooperate or be his normal stubborn self? Would our conversation evolve into a heated argument or would the evening end calmly? Would we go to the hospital?

I turned into the gravel driveway and parked. My headlights lit the white siding of the manufactured home and anxiousness swept over me. There was never any way to know what I would face in an encounter with him.

The garage broke up the face of the house like a black hole. Jose had left the garage door up for me and the inside back door unlocked, so I could enter with ease.

"Just come on in," Jose had said over the phone.

Tonight felt eerie, but at the same time comforting, almost as if the house said *Welcome home*. Not eager to draw attention too quickly, I slowly turned the doorknob to the entryway and tugged gently. That door always made a noise. The house was dark except for the glow of the overhead stove night light that shone dimly across the open kitchen.

I softly walked down the dark narrow entry, past the washer and dryer in the laundry room, and stepped into the kitchen. Flickering light and muffled sounds came from Jose's TV quietly playing in his bedroom at the far end of the double-wide home.

Glancing at the clock on the stove, I was surprised to see it was 10:00 p.m., yet the TV in the living room was off. He didn't normally go to bed until 11:00 p.m. or after. Though the living room was dark, a stream of light came from his bedroom on the other side of the kitchen. Peering into the room, I saw him sitting on the edge of the mattress and massaging lotion onto his legs.

"Hi there." I hovered at the bedroom door, waiting to see his response to my surprise visit.

He glanced up. "Well," his tone reflected surprise bordering on being pleased to see me. "What are you doing here?"

Relieved there was no immediate backlash, I gently sat beside him. We faced his dresser that hugged the wall close enough in front of us I could reach and touch it. A single lamp on the bedside table made a small circle of light. I sat close, feeling the warmth of his body next to mine. My heart sank when I noticed his legs were grossly swollen. Now I understood why Jose was worried.

"Well…" I spoke softly. "Jose called and was very concerned about you."

"That Jose," he snapped. "He didn't need to call you. I'm fine."

"Your legs are swollen pretty bad." I nodded to the cream in his hands. "Tell me what's going on."

He listed his current health challenges. With each item, I grew more anxious.

"I'm really concerned about you," I summarized. "And so is Jose. I think it would be a good idea if we go to the hospital and just have them check things out."

"Not tonight." He shook his head. "We'll go in the morning."

The fact he agreed to go at all proved to me even he was concerned about what was happening to his body. "Okay," I agreed, "but I'm not leaving you."

"Crawl into the other side of the bed," he said.

I considered sleeping on the couch but worried he might not make it through the night. I wanted to stay close, so I could hear him if he needed me.

Sleep didn't come easy that night. While he slept, I lay beside him and prayed to God he'd grant us time to get him to the hospital before it was too late. The love that still lingered in my heart peaked and rose to the surface.

The next day's diagnosis was bad news. He had sepsis in his blood, infection spreading to other areas of his body, and his kidneys were failing. I stayed with him at the hospital as much as I could, while running back and forth to my own printing business, which was forty-five minutes away.

I opened *The Cause Printing Company* in a city close by while we were still married to help raise funds for the non-profit I founded called *Crossroad Connections*. The idea was to *print for a purpose,* and the profits supported our outreach projects including building a wheelchair ramp for a double amputee with spina-bifida and hosting other community outreach events. We organized clothing trades, toy trades at Christmas time, and the *Back-to-School Blast* with fun carnival games where the kids won school supplies as prizes.

I was the only one who could do the manual screen printing of the T-shirts people ordered, so I went to work long enough each day to get the printing done, and then left the other duties in the care of my employees.

Juggling this new schedule became taxing, and he became more demanding of my time as his needs increased.

At the hospital one evening, I stood with my back turned away from him while I wrote on the dry erase board on the wall across from his bed.

"You're losing weight," he said.

Still writing, I answered. "Yes, I've lost twenty pounds."

"Why are you doing that?" From his tone, I suspected he thought I was trying to get the attention of a new guy.

"I'm not trying. It's just happening." I added, "They found out that I have Graves' disease."

"They what?" His voice rose in that high-pitched way he used when he didn't agree with something.

"Bloodwork showed I have Graves' disease," I explained. "My thyroid isn't functioning right."

He never asked anymore about my health. When we were married, he didn't believe me when I kept saying I felt exhausted, had no energy, my muscles were weak, and I trembled and couldn't stand after squatting to apply graphics on a vehicle.

When I reported I could hear my heartbeat pounding at an abnormal rate when I went to bed, he made snide remarks. "Yeah, Valerie, just keep going to the doctor. One day they'll find something wrong with you."

I didn't tell him the doctors felt the Graves' disease was my body's response to the stress of our marriage. The severe tension eventually destroyed my thyroid's ability to function properly. Graves' disease was rare, they said.

When he came home from the hospital, Home Healthcare nurses arrived each day to give his medicines and injections.

Before long, he refused to let the nurses do the injections. Instead, he insisted I was the only one he'd allow to administer the shots. Later, his illness began to affect his mind and hallucinations took over.

A few days into my new routine of driving to his house each morning, I arrived to give him the injections. I once again removed the cold glass vials of medicine from the refrigerator door. He sat in his recliner as he often had while we were married, except now he was pretty much confined because he could no longer walk on his own. From the living room, he initiated an argument with me in the kitchen.

"Those vials are not supposed to be in the refrigerator." He went on to argue about which medications to use, how much, and when.

I filled the syringes the way the nurse had shown me and went to the corner of the living room where he sat rocking. I flicked the syringe with my fingers to remove any air bubbles, released a drop of the fluid, and twisted the end into his port tube to administer the medicine with one slow push of the plunger.

He looked straight, his eyes stone cold. "You're probably poisoning me."

I wasn't sure where that idea came from, but I thought he was trying to be funny. I responded half-jokingly, half-sarcastic, "Yes, I am poisoning you." Frustration lingering from our previous conversation, I felt annoyed I was there to help him, but he was making it difficult.

I went to work for the day and later learned he seriously imagined I was trying to poison him. He called the sheriff's department out to his house where he reported I was trying to kill him. That's when I knew it was no longer safe for me to be around him. I needed to step away. I called his son and sister and told them they would have to take care of him. I couldn't keep caring for him under the circumstances.

I felt bad for them. I felt bad for him. None of this was easy on anyone. I was determined to find other ways to help him.

The hallucinations got worse. His anger grew to dangerous levels. One evening, Jose came home from work and walked into a tirade because Jose had forgotten to set the trash out to the road that morning. He called Jose terrible names, stumbled to his bedroom closet, pulled out a shotgun, and propped the gun by his recliner while threatening the life of the young man he once called his best friend.

Jose was so frightened, he phoned his brother who drove to the house. Jose and his brother loaded Jose's belongings into his brother's truck, and Jose moved out that night. He not only lost his roommate and best friend that evening, but he also lost his lead screen printer for the company. Jose had no intention of having any connection with someone who threatened to kill him.

The vicious cycle of crazy episodes and hallucinations continued as he remained alone at home. One evening, he thought Jose was taunting him and having a party in his neighbor's yard.

His condition went from affecting his home life and personal relationships to filtering into his business. He thought he had become rich and began to buy equipment the company couldn't afford. Other employees tried to step in to fill Jose's place as the screen printer, but the quality and organization of the company began to fall apart. Long-time customers became angry and took their business elsewhere. Sales plummeted.

When I learned of the decline of the business, I started sneaking into the office every day. My goal was to help his business partner stop and reverse the damage his illness had on his company without him knowing I was there. I made phone calls to sales reps I knew to stop trucks from leaving the docks that had new equipment he had ordered already loaded and ready to ship to our location. I worked late at night printing as much as I could and still ran to my own company forty-five minutes away to print there as well. My employees were feeling the pressure as they tried to pick up my slack when I was at his business instead of mine.

He was homebound for a period, but once he could drive, I'd have to slip out the back door of his business if he unexpectedly showed up. My heart broke for him. He had worked too hard to lose it all, and I prayed he'd recover soon, and things would return to normal.

Notwithstanding, there remained a major problem. He was not getting back to normal, and things grew more intense. Employees no longer wanted to come into work because they were afraid of him. He purchased a brand new shiny black truck with all the add-ons available. The family and I knew he couldn't afford it. Somewhere, somehow, we had to get him help.

CHAPTER EIGHT

Lighthouse Keeper

After he returned home from the hospital, his youngest son and I worked well together to care for his needs. With a family and young children of his own as well as a full-time job, his son had a lot to do in addition to helping with his father. When I had to step away from the house, his son provided care. We took turns checking in and taking him to doctor appointments.

As our concern for his well-being grew, his sister suggested we ask the police if we could do anything to prevent him from coming into the office. His mental health was not stable, and it was affecting everyone. We wanted to know if we could force him to go to the hospital and get checked out, or in this case, get checked in.

His sister, his mom, and I drove downtown to the sheriff's department. We entered the foyer doors that were tinted with one-way glass. We crossed the small lobby that contained two rows of chairs and four phone booths used for families to talk to inmates. The three of us approached the small office window.

His sister spoke to the woman on the other side of the glass. "Can we speak to an officer, please?"

The receptionist told us to have a seat, and she would send someone out to talk with us.

The three of us sat in the blue plastic seats that reminded me of chairs from a school.

His sister spoke to me. "Are you glad you're no longer married to him?"

I was shocked at the question, but quick to answer. "Yes, I believe God was protecting me." I had often considered that exact question as the situation had gotten worse between us. I couldn't imagine what life would have been like if my boys and I still lived there with his current condition.

"But if you were married," his mom interjected, "you could have gotten him the help he needs."

"You're right, that is true." I felt bad I spoke so quickly in front of his mother. I knew her heart was broken as she watched her son go through this illness. I knew how much it hurt me to watch his decline. And there is no love like a mother's.

We had not waited long before the locked steel door clicked and opened. Out came two officers in their tan and brown uniforms, shiny gold star badges were pinned at their chests.

"Hello, ladies," said one of the officers. "How can we help you?"

"Oh," his sister squealed excitedly. "I'm so glad to see you. I hoped we would be able to talk to you guys."

I recognized the sheriff and his captain. I knew both men personally from the years when my father served as a deputy for the department. I went to high school and had become friends with the young man who was now the captain. Both men had been customers at our business.

"We happened to both be in the office when they said some ladies were in the lobby needing help," said Captain Chris. "We decided we would both come see how we could help."

They invited us to follow them through the heavy door that locked behind us. Down the narrow hall, we were ushered into a small room with a long table. The three of us women took seats on one side, and the guys sat on the other, facing us.

The tall, dark-haired sheriff with wired-rimmed glasses, sat across from me. "What can we do for you, ladies?"

We shared some of the events that had taken place and our concern for my ex-husband's medical condition and his business. The guys listened to everything we had to say and displayed compassion for our situation.

"He even thought I was trying to poison him," I related.

"I know." Captain Chris nodded his head. "I was the officer who drove out to his house when he called the department. By the things he said, I knew something wasn't quite right. We stood in the driveway for quite a while talking." I was thankful Chris knew me well enough to know those accusations weren't true. The police had not even called me in for questioning.

"Is there anything we can do legally to get him into the hospital? Something is seriously medically wrong," I said. "I'm afraid I'll find him dead." I lowered my voice. "Or someone else."

"Are you still married?" The sheriff wanted to know. "Or is your divorce final?"

"No, we aren't married. It's all final." My heart sank, feeling weighed down by hopelessness.

"If it wasn't final yet, and you were still legally married, you could get him into the hospital," the sheriff explained. "You would have that right as his guardian. I'm really sorry, but there isn't much we can legally do to help you. This is a tough one. Valerie, I would advise that you go to an attorney and get guardianship over him if you are willing."

We thanked them for their time and guidance. His sister and mother and I left with a plan to go together and seek counsel from an attorney. Perhaps there was still something helpful that could be done.

The following week, we met with an attorney. She recommended I take on the responsibility of establishing guardianship, so we could get the help he so badly needed before something terrible happened.

In the next couple of weeks, a new battle arose. I was running my business from afar, still striving to save his company, working countless hours under extreme pressure, and taking care of my two boys who lived with me. All the while, I worried something crazy or terrible was about to happen with *him*.

The attorney phoned out of the blue and asked me to come to her office right away. "There has been a new development," she said.

I drove downtown wondering what could require my immediate presence in her office. Inside the lobby, surrounded by the old-style wood paneling, the secretary greeted me with a smile. "She will be right with you," the secretary said. "She is expecting you."

Minutes later, the tall, slender, attractive lady appeared and motioned me back to her office. With anticipation, I sat in the chair in front of her big wooden desk.

"The family's attorney called me," she began. "His oldest son doesn't want you to have guardianship. Apparently, your ex-husband is still terrified of you. They asked if you'd be willing to drop your request."

"What about the care he needs?"

"They will get guardianship of him."

You've got to be kidding me. My thoughts tumbled over each other. *Why didn't they bother getting guardianship earlier to give their father the care he needed? Why are they fighting me now? Is this out of spite?*

I took a breath and considered. The goal was to have someone oversee his care.

"I don't care who has guardianship," I told her. "I only did this to get help for him before something bad happens."

"Their attorney is waiting for me to call him back. I'll get him on the line." She picked up the phone and dialed.

"Who is going to take care of him?"

She met my gaze. "Let's find out."

She continued to make eye contact with me as she spoke on the phone. "Valerie is asking who is going to take care of him?"

From her conversation, I gathered the couple and my ex were in the other attorney's office at that moment. My attorney relayed the message he gave her from the other end. "He wants his daughter-in-law to take care of him."

He was a sick man, but he wasn't so sick that he wasn't capable of still trying to manipulate. He knew his daughter-in-law and I were not each other's favorite people. I doubted the daughter-in-law was aware of how he spoke about her to me. He had talked badly about her for years, but now *he* wanted *her* to take care of him?

"That's fine," I calmly agreed. "All I want is for them to get him the help he needs. Are they going to do that? Will they get him in to see a doctor?"

Through the attorney's phone I could hear his attorney on the other end. "All Ms. Juillerat wants is for him to get the help he needs."

They agreed to take him to the doctor, and I agreed to sign off and no longer pursue guardianship. I walked out of the office with a bill for $900 for trying to take care of a man who was no longer my husband. Ironically, he now wanted the person he couldn't stand to oversee his medical care rather than having me do this for him. She was about to find out what he was really like.

Less than twenty-four hours later, my cell phone rang. Standing at the manual press, I was in the process of printing an order of T-shirts for a customer. The print room was hot and noisy with the fan and dryer running. To better hear, I stepped into a back room which he had previously used as his old office.

"Hello," I answered. "This is Valerie."

"Valerie, their attorney just called." I recognized the voice of my attorney. "I'm really sorry to have to tell you this, but they've taken him to the hospital. The daughter-in-law called this morning, and he wouldn't answer. She drove to the house and found him in bed. He was unresponsive."

She paused. "Their attorney thought you should know. You tried getting him help, Valerie. You did all you could do. I'm really sorry."

"Thank you," I choked past the lump that suddenly swelled in my throat. "And thank you for calling."

In one sense, I felt relief. He was now in the hospital where he could hopefully get good medical care that might help him be better. On the other hand, I felt sad, worried about his condition. Had his trip to the hospital come too late?

He wanted *faith* to be enough to heal him. He didn't want people to know his condition because he felt like their prayers, coming from fear, were not the prayers he wanted to be prayed over him. He wanted prayers of faith and trust for his healing. And for people to actually believe in what they prayed for to come to fruition. He didn't seek medical treatment because he wanted his healing to come from God Almighty Himself. He may have been a hard man, but he did love the Lord and believed in Him with all his being.

I heard a sermon one time by one of *his* favorite pastors and tried to encourage him to listen to the message. "If your sink is leaking, you call the plumber to fix it. If your roof is leaking, you call the roofer to fix it. You don't sit on the rooftop saying, 'I'm waiting for God to fix it.' He gives us doctors, medicine, and resources to help care for us. He gave people the knowledge and wisdom to do what they do, just like Luke, the physician named in the scriptures. We do our part, too. You can't just sit on the roof waiting for God to do it all. Yes, pray for healing, and do your part."

I shared with him the religious man's joke shared by the same pastor. The story goes that a religious man is on top of a roof during a great flood.

A man comes by in a boat and says, "Get in, get in!"

The religious man replies, "No, I have faith in God, he will grant me a miracle."

Later, when the water had risen to his waist, another boat comes by. "Get into my boat," the captain urges.

But the man on the roof responds that he has faith in God, and God will give him a miracle.

When the water reaches chest-high, another boat comes to rescue him, but he turns down the offer again because "God will grant a miracle."

With the water up to his chin, a helicopter hovers overhead and throws down a ladder. "Grab the ladder and climb into the helicopter," they tell him.

Mumbling with the water in his mouth, he turns down the offer for help from the helicopter. "My God will save me," he says.

Soon after, the man arrives at the gates of Heaven. "I thought God would grant me a miracle," he tells Peter. "I have been let down."

Peter responds, "I don't know what you're complaining about, we sent you three boats and a helicopter."

I often wonder if he had sought medical help early on, how differently things would have turned out for him. Our God the Creator *can and still does* perform miracles, He *can and still does* heal, or He can simply choose to provide. We can do our part to partner with God and trust him with the outcome.

We had two business locations at the time, one where we did the printing production, and the other location served as the storefront, offices, and graphics production rooms. I had gone downtown to work on graphics, and his sister was in the office catching up on bookwork. Both of us waited for news about his condition.

The phone rang, and the next thing I knew, his sister came into the production room where I was bent over the large graphics worktable, weeding out vinyl for decals.

She gently removed the X-acto knife from my hand and laid it on the table. "They just called," she said softly. "He's in a coma."

I broke like a dam. Exhaustion, the feeling of defeat and letdown, knowing how hard I tried to slow the progression of the illness, how I longed to prevent *this* exact situation, all of these emotions washed over me like a tidal wave. I had never cried that hard in front of anyone in all my life.

"I know that you still love him." She placed her hand on my back while I leaned over the table. In the middle of that large room, we shared tears for a man we loved despite his imperfections.

During his period of hallucinations, he had told his family all kinds of horrible untruths about me. His sister tried to negate the accusations and explain how bad his mindset had been recently. She tried to protect my heart by not letting me know what all was said. She knew me and knew these untruths were part of the hallucinations. She reminded family members he also said he saw Jose partying in his neighbor's backyard when Jose was never there.

I asked what room he was in at the hospital, but his son refused to allow me to see him. I waited until I knew no one would be around and drove the forty miles in traffic to the hospital. Quietly, I slipped into his room. I needed to see him. I needed closure in case I never got to see him alive again. And I *needed* to pray over him.

The first night, I went to his room and stood near his bed. I hoped he would hear my voice and open his eyes even for just a moment. I placed my hand on his arm and prayed for his healing. A nurse popped in and saw me standing there. She smiled and went about her business.

The next night, I stood at his bedside when a nurse approached and asked gruffly, "Who are you?"

"I was married to him," I responded.

"You need to leave," she snapped.

"I was his wife," I replied sternly while trying to remain calm and kind to her.

"You need to leave now," she said. "His son told us we are not to let you in."

I walked to the blue loveseat under the window and grabbed the strap to my purse. While the nurse watched, I walked by the bed and touched his arm one last time. "Goodbye, honey. I love you."

I brushed past her at the door and left the building. Anger boiled inside me as I walked back to my car. After I worked so hard to try to help him and save his business, this was the appreciation I received.

During the one-hour drive back home, I prayed he would survive this. What would tonight be like if his family had been this concerned about his well-being *before* it came to this?

The hospital stay was long and tough for him, followed by an extended stay in a rehabilitation facility. With him safely taken care of now, I told his sister it was time for me to step back from their company. I had my own business to manage. Perhaps she could manage his business and keep the company together now that he wouldn't be working against her.

CHAPTER NINE

Lighthouse Beacon

T he final weekend of September dawned clear and crisp for the Pioneer Festival at the fairgrounds. The annual autumn event remained a favorite of mine with high-spirited attendees in pioneer costumes and the seasonal foods of pulled pork, hot apple cider, and kettles of caramel corn.

As a Community and Family Services board member, I helped sell giant smoked turkey legs, hot apple cider, and cold drinks as a fundraiser for the homeless shelter. The old wooden booth was decorated to look period-correct complete with strategically placed cornstalks, pumpkins, and a handwritten chalkboard menu.

David had not been listening very well the week before. As a result, he was grounded from seeing his friends for the weekend. Instead, he helped in the booth handing out drinks and collecting money. He was only allowed to walk around the festival with me on our breaks.

We had costume requirements, so I wore my full-length, royal blue dress and black round-tipped boots. My grandmother's beautiful ivory lace shawl draped across my shoulders.

On Sunday, the last day of the festival, David and I took a break from the booth to walk through the festival grounds. We saw tents with hand-carved tools, booths with wooden toys, and traders offered animal furs and leathers. Campfires blazed under black kettles of simmering food. The aroma of smoked meats and corn on the cob filled the air.

At our favorite tent, a local church served homemade apple dumplings topped with vanilla ice cream. We purchased one for each of us and took our treat to the old green picnic tables in the nearby pavilions. As a nine-year veteran of 4-H, those tables always brought back memories of summers at the fairgrounds with my friends.

Even though David was grounded, I enjoyed having him with me and sharing this time with just the two of us. His blue T-shirt made his beautiful blue eyes pop against his blonde hair. His cheeks were rosy from the heat. Watching him enjoy his ice cream made me smile. We talked and people-watched until we licked the last drop of ice cream from our spoons, knowing we wouldn't get another one of these delicious desserts until next year's festival.

Next, David and I walked the paths of trampled grass and straw, taking our time to leisurely explore the historical exhibits.

I noticed a dark-haired gentleman in sunglasses, an orange polo shirt, and khaki shorts. I wondered why that nice-looking guy was walking around by himself. He carried a small brown bag and appeared to be taking his time to take in the sights.

David and I stopped to listen to a group of musicians. While we stood there listening, the man in the orange shirt walked up and leaned against a nearby maple tree. Then I realized I knew him. His name was Mark, and we had attended the same high school. Though I never got to know him on a personal level, even back then he had caught my eye. I remember him in the library during study hall and thinking how quiet he was. But now, I knew something else about him. Something sad.

A mutual friend had recently shared about Mark's devastating heartbreak. Previously, I had attended church with his wife though we never had the chance to get close. We were friends on Facebook, and her pictures portrayed them as a happy couple. I recall staring at one particular photo, thinking how lucky she was to be so happily married. They had been married for more than twenty-five years, something I always wanted to achieve, but I didn't know if I would ever reach that milestone in this lifetime. Now, my heart hurt for him because he was alone.

David and I made another loop around the park, and as we came to the place where the musicians continued to play, I saw Mark was still there.

My heart sped up, and I knew I was to say specific words to him. "David, I need to tell this guy something."

My son gave me a questioning look and followed.

As I approached Mark, I noticed he had lost a lot of weight. Yet, I was certain it was him behind those dark sunglasses. "Mark? Are you Mark?" I asked as I extended my hand toward him.

"Well, yes, I am." He answered and took my hand and gently cupped it in his.

Chills went down my spine at his tender touch and the way he held my hand. No one had done that to me before.

"I just wanted to tell you, I'm sorry. I heard about you and your wife." I went on to explain. "I used to be friends with her. I am so very sorry for what you are going through."

"Used to be friends." He chuckled with a note of irony.

"We used to go to the same church," I said. "But I no longer go there."

"And your name is?"

"I'm Valerie."

"Well, thank you, Valerie," he said. "I appreciate your kind words."

"You're welcome," I told him as I began to step away. "You take care now."

"Thank you." He nodded to David and me.

Leaving Mark alone at the maple tree, David and I walked back to the turkey leg booth. I asked if the director needed our help. The lines of customers had dwindled, and there were plenty of other volunteers to serve the occasional patron. Since they didn't need me until closing when they would need help tearing down, David and I were free to wander the festival some more.

"Let's go listen to the music for a bit," I suggested to David. We walked back along the curved path, stopping to talk to a few friends along the way. When the tent where the musicians played came into view, I saw the orange shirt vibrantly standing out against the dark background of the tree.

A new prompting rose up in me. "David, watch and learn," I told him as we reapproached the man at the tree.

"We're going to sit and listen to the music," I said to Mark as we walked past him. "Would you like to join us?"

"Sure." He followed us to a bench.

For the next half hour, the music served as background to our conversation. Mark appeared completely oblivious to the performers while he poured out his heart. I felt bad for the musicians because he talked above them, but I listened to both. The musicians were talented, and I felt it was evident the man needed to talk.

After the band played their last song, the three of us stood and walked out of the tent. During the conversation, we learned we were both single and alone.

"Well, thank you for letting me join you," he said. "And for listening to me babble."

"You're welcome." I smiled.

"Would you mind giving me your number?" He reached up and removed his sunglasses. "Maybe we could go out to eat sometime. There is no sense in both of us eating alone, now is there?"

"Sure." If nothing else, I thought the poor guy needed a friend to talk to.

It had been almost a year since my divorce. I had gone on dates with a few guys, but I hadn't found anyone I seemed to connect with or someone I desired to have a long-term relationship with. A couple of weeks earlier I had prayed and told God, "I don't want to do the dating game anymore, Lord. Bring me your chosen one for me. Bring me the appointed one."

I didn't expect to ever hear from him, but two weeks later he phoned. "Hello, Valerie, this is Mark. We met at the Pioneer Festival, and you gave me your number."

I remembered. "Oh, well hello, Mark."

"We had talked about getting together sometime," he said nervously. "I wanted to know if you would be interested in going out?"

We made plans to go to another festival the following weekend. We had to drive quite a distance to get there, which gave us time to get to know one another. This was a large festival with a lot of people in attendance. I had never been to this one before, so it was new and exciting.

We enjoyed meandering through the craft booths and other displays. Sitting on a bench and eating an ice cream cone felt like a real date. Something magical I hadn't experienced in a really long time.

A rain cloud darkened the sky above, and raindrops dampened our shirts. We jogged up to a big red barn at the top of a small hill. Inside was crowded with people trying to get out of the rain. The center area was packed with tables holding handmade crafts and flea market goods. We wove through the booths while the rain continued.

He noticed three compact umbrellas on one of the tables. "Which one would you like?"

I selected one, and he took it to an older woman who tended the booth. She smiled almost like she knew there was something special about us as he paid her three dollars for the umbrella. This was the first time I noticed such a look from someone.

He opened the umbrella and carried it over me as we walked through the crowd and back to his truck. Then the rain stopped and down came the umbrella. We continued to work our way toward the exit. There was so much congestion, at one point he followed behind instead of walking beside me. I looked over my shoulder to make sure he was still close by. Then there was a touch on my back. An unexpected sensation flowed through me.

When we got to the truck, I asked if he had touched my back while we were walking.

"Well, yes," he replied. "I did."

I knew there was something special about him, about us, right then. There was only one other time I felt something similar, and that was when I touched another person in church when I put my hand on a man's back. Not knowing the heartache he had just gone through, I could literally feel his pain as I prayed over him.

The next weekend we went to another festival on another date. This time we brought my boys along, so they could get to know Mark and he could get to know them. The boys were polite and well-behaved except when a sibling fight occasionally broke out, so I wasn't worried about taking them along on a date.

It was another beautiful autumn day, and we enjoyed the tents and exhibits, and the boys played a game of tug-of-war. We bought glass bottles of homemade root beer that we drank on our walk along the dirt road back to his truck.

The boys chatted and walked a few yards ahead of Mark and me. Surrounded by the cool woods on both sides of us, I carried my root beer bottle I wanted to keep for memory's sake in one hand and the other hand swung free at my side.

The last eight months of marriage to my ex-husband, he never touched me. No hugs, no holding hands, no kisses, and no intimacy. Mark's touch felt like it was in slow motion as his fingers slowly slid down my hand until he cupped my hand in his. Romantic touch. Something I had not felt in a long while.

David glanced back and did a double-take. He grinned. Turning back, he shared his observation with his brother, and they giggled.

CHAPTER TEN

The Rainbow

My ex-husband's business partner telephoned. "Valerie, he asked me to call and ask if you would like to buy the company."

My heart grasped at the words. Was this the answer to my prayers?

"He is just too sick to come back in and run it," his partner continued. "And I have no desire to do it. He said that if anyone could turn this thing back around, it would be you."

That was my dream business I had walked away from during the divorce. "Yes," I quickly responded. "I would like to buy the business."

God provided a way for me to purchase the company, which became a Christmas gift to myself. New challenges came along as part of the package deal. I worked long, hard hours to repair the damage and rebuild what had once been a half-million dollar company. Sales continued to drop for about another year, and then I was able to finally get them to level out and stay steady for two solid years.

Life was good. Really good! I had my dream house, my dream business and I had met this great guy. From that very first weekend, he was everything I had been looking for, handsome, funny, compassionate, and he loved my Lord. We shared interests in movies, festivals, pizza, and traveling adventures. We both enjoyed writing, painting, and creativity. He constantly made me laugh, and laughing was something I hadn't had much of for a long time.

He had an amazing heart of compassion and became my biggest encourager. What I believed entwined our hearts the most was our love for God. I had never had a spiritual connection with anyone before.

I felt I had found my soulmate. When we had dated for nine months, everyone thought we'd be getting married. Including me.

CHAPTER ELEVEN

Dreamers

A black mass rolled and roiled overhead.

Was a storm coming our way? The intimidating thunderhead swirled and rotated like a tornado bearing down.

But the darkness deepened. Threatened. What was this really? A winter storm brewing or something much more powerful and dangerous. Something evil.

I couldn't tear my eyes away as the form expanded, swirled, and drew near. With a low growl, this dark presence swooped toward me. Picking up speed, it rushed forward like a freight train. I held my breath in fear as it dropped lower. Closer.

Inches from touching me, I felt its breath. Like the voice that taunted me when I was a teenager pushing through the narrow black tunnels of a haunted house, I heard the haughty laugh.

"Hahahaha. I'm coming after you."

Squeezing my eyes tightly closed, I quickly turned my head away. I pressed myself back, dreading its touch on my skin. As the frightening presence reached for me, I screamed a cry for help with the only word I could get out.

"Jesus!"

I awoke, sitting straight up in bed.

This was the first of a sequence of spiritual dreams that occurred during this season of my life. Some were demonic like this one where demons warned of their intentions, but then came the dreams from God, preparing me with strength and courage for the things to come. I embraced *His* plans for me.

In this tug-of-war between good and evil, my sons and I were the targets. I was called to be the lady warrior, dressed in armor, holding a shiny silver sword at the ready. I needed to gear up for a battle of darkness. God intended for me to stand and fight.

I could always tell a spiritual dream versus my brain's natural sensory processing. The spiritual dreams had a feeling of great importance or warning. These vital visions happened in the early morning hours. I could remember every detail while only snippets remained in my memory of less significant dreams. Despite trouble with short-term memory, the vividness of these dreams was outstanding.

Some I understood immediately, and others required two years before God revealed their meaning to me. After time lapsed and I forgot about the images, God brought the visuals of the dream back to my memory like watching a video replay. He showed me the link between the here and now and the dream He gave to me earlier as the event took place.

My Grandpa Virgil was a pastor. I recall he shared his visions and dreams with me while I was a young girl. One day, sitting at the supper table with Grandpa and Grandma, Grandpa Virgil told me about the day he saw angels in his orchard. Grandma Chella and I listened intently; our eyes glued on Grandpa.

"I was in the orchard picking pears," he described. "I heard voices coming down the road toward the house. I thought some kids were on their bikes on the other side of the hill, but I couldn't see them yet. The sound continued to get louder. I looked over toward the chatter again, and up over the hill came what looked like a cloud gliding up the road. I watched the cloud come into the orchard toward me. I heard the voices of two ladies, but I couldn't physically see their image. They laughed and talked."

Giddy, Grandpa smiled, and the emotion caused his eyes to squint. "I couldn't make out what they said. The angels crossed right in front of me as I stood at the pear tree. They glided across the yard and continued along the road until they faded out of sight. That next week, the local newspaper reported that others described seeing the same thing in the park."

"Wow," I said with childlike amazement. "I wish I could see angels."

Knowing these things as a young girl, I didn't feel my dreams made me odd or different, but as I got older, the dreams made me feel alone at times because there were very few people I knew that could relate to my experiences.

I'll never forget the astonished look on Mark's face the first time I shared about some of my dreams with him.

"Wow," he said. "I haven't met many others who are like me. Normally, when I tell people about my dreams, they look at me like I have a third eye."

I understood that feeling. I had stopped sharing much with people because they reacted as if I were strange or being oddly over-spiritual.

The words of Acts 2:17 (NIV) brought comfort. "In the last days, God says, I will pour out my Spirit on all people. Your sons and daughters will prophesy, your young men will see visions, your old men will dream dreams."

When I nervously shared my story with a publishing agent, I was shocked at her response. "Oh, Valerie, you are very special. God showed you these things ahead of time to prepare your heart."

Her words brought tears to my eyes. She helped me to view the dreams as God's gift.

When the agent shared her beautiful thoughts, they triggered a memory of my Grandma Chella who was one of the most precious and influential people of my life. The week before her stroke that would take her life a month later, Grandma sat in her oversized, burgundy, rocker-recliner and watched one of her daytime soap operas. She described how the TV suddenly went black as if the station went off the air. Then a man appeared on the screen and simply stated, "Something big is about to happen." The screen flipped back to black for a moment and returned to her regular program.

God granted Grandma a vision and allowed her to prepare for what was to come next in her life. She picked up the phone and was able to call most of her seven children to talk to them. Grandma knew whatever the man's message would mean; it was important.

Shortly after, the stroke caused her to fall to the green tile on the bathroom floor. She never recovered enough to speak to her children again.

The agent said I was special to God. God thought my Grandma Chella was special, too.

CHAPTER TWELVE

Storm Fatalities

On Black Friday, I shopped with my aunt, sister-in-law, and mother.

We hunted for sales, compared prices, and checked items off our lists on our Christmas shopping spree. The van was packed with small and large packages we had competed with the wild crowd to buy. On the way home, we dropped off my aunt at her house before parking in the stony driveway at my parents' home.

"Before we go in," I spoke up, "I want to tell you about a dream I had."

Mom took her hand off the door handle and turned to listen. Melissa leaned forward from the back seat to better hear my story.

"I was standing in a village in the dusty desert of another country," I began. "Beside the homes of those who lived there, a camp was set up consisting of canvas tents and bare tree limbs."

The next part was difficult to say. "Dead bodies were lying on the ground everywhere across the camp. There were so many dead people the children ran and played over the bodies."

Eyes wide, my mom and sister-in-law listened intently. "I held my breath, afraid to breathe in death until I heard the voice of the

Holy Spirit say, 'Don't worry, I will protect you.' I trusted the voice. But why had I traveled all that way there? While I peered over the lifeless bodies in the village, a dark-skinned little boy whose features made me think he was a native of Africa, ran to me. He stopped and silently stared me straight in the face. Sensing he wanted me to follow him, I took a step forward. He turned and ran toward a tent a little way ahead of us. He stopped midway down the path and looked back over his shoulder to be certain I followed."

Taking a breath, I continued. "When we reached the tent opening, I stepped inside to total darkness. From the center of the space, I looked to the opening to see the boy standing in the doorway. Though I beckoned, he wouldn't cross the threshold and enter. His expression seemed to say he had accomplished his mission and was satisfied I was there. Then he ran away as quickly as he had come.

"In the darkness, I tried to adjust my eyes. What I thought I saw to my left was a bed against the tent wall. Assuming someone was sick, and the boy had brought me here to help, I approached the place. To my surprise, there was no bed. Instead, I suddenly felt a supernatural presence of evil. Mounds of dark body forms consumed the bottom of the tent wall. As if awakening, the forms moved like a wave.

"'Jesus!'" I yelled so loudly I woke from the dream. My heart raced. For a long time, I could not go back to sleep."

My sister-in-law shook her head. "I would not be able to sleep after that either. What do you think is the meaning of the dream?"

"I'm certain this was a dream from God," I replied. "And someday I'm going to another country. Though I'm not certain, I think I will help find a way to feed their people."

While I was in the dream, I rationalized why I was there. At that time, I was in the process of building my nonprofit organization called *Crossroad Connections*. One aspect of the foundation was teaching people how to budget for food through a method I called

35 for 4. My board and I were in discussions about starting a food pantry.

Additionally, Mark was considering partnering with a family member's ministry to come up with ways food could be grown in the desert and on unnourished ground. These facts combined with the images of my dream, so my first impression was the dream confirmed I could help people secure a source for food. I was there in the village to feed the people and help prevent them from dying.

"I have no doubt God is speaking to me through this dream and preparing me to do something for others," I said to my mom and sister-in-law.

However, two years passed before I understood the what, where, when, and how. The purpose became clear when pictures on a projection screen brought me to tears, and God revealed His direction.

Meanwhile, life was good these days.

I owned my dream business. Mark brought new excitement and adventure into my life, and the boys liked him. My dream home had become just that, a peaceful and safe place for my boys and me. My heart felt full and free to love again.

One morning, I stood at the sink in the master bathroom putting on my makeup to get ready for work. David peeked around the corner through the open door. Seeing him in the mirror, I grinned and waved him to join me. He leaned against the bathroom counter, and we chatted.

David watched through the reflection in the mirror as I applied foundation to my face.

I opened the little plastic container that held my eye shadow. Using the sponge brush applicator, I swept the fine light blue powder across my eyelid.

"Let me do it."

I met his gaze in the mirror. "Let you do my makeup?"

"Yeah."

I handed the little black brush to him and closed my eyes. He dipped the applicator into the colored powder and gently pressed the eye shadow to my eyelid as he'd seen me do countless times before.

He considered his work. "There," he affirmed proudly.

I turned to the mirror and inspected his work. "Good job."

Standing behind me, he reached his tween arms around my shoulders and locked his arms in front of me. "Te amo, Mama." He translated his Spanish, "I love you, Mama."

"I love you too, Davie."

Life in that moment felt perfect.

CHAPTER THIRTEEN

Drug Gales

To advertise his son's new carpet cleaning business, the father of Austin's best friend inquired about having vinyl graphics lettering for the sides of his van.

Once the layout and design were approved, the vinyl was cut and ready to install. The weather was clear and warm, so there was no need for a garage or shelter. After closing the shop, I planned to go to his house to complete the job that evening.

I pulled up to his address in the silver company vehicle. The little truck held the tools I needed, including the long pieces of shiny-black vinyl prepped with transfer tape. Splashed with my own company graphics, the truck made me feel equipped and empowered to do my job well.

I turned into the drive, viewing the rundown little house that needed a good power washing and a fresh coat of paint. Though inside the city limits, the property carried an air of being in the country. The lush green tree line grew along the side of the dirt driveway. From the repeated passage of vehicle wheels, ruts had molded tracks into the drive that lay muddy from recent spring rain.

Austin and the boy who lived here had been friends and schoolmates for several years. He was a stalky, blonde-haired teen who was always extremely polite and had quickly come to comfortably call me Mom. Being aware his relationship with his own mother wasn't particularly easy, I was intentional in showing love and kindness to him.

I put the truck in park and got out of the vehicle. A heavy-set man came out of the back screen door of the house.

He smiled broadly. "It's Mom!" He gave me a bear hug. "Hi, Mom, it's nice to finally meet you in person."

I welcomed the job, but I wasn't feeling so easy about his embrace. The boys had told me I had caught the man's eye, and he was taking a fond interest in me. Though single and lonely, I couldn't say I felt the same in return for him.

I quickly went into business mode and said I was ready to install the vinyl work. He led me to the van parked crosswise in the yard at the front of the house. I grabbed my black tool bag and the pieces of taped-up, oddly shaped decals that had been neatly stretched out on the floor of the back of the truck.

As soon as I began the installation, he said he needed to leave, got in his car, and drove away. Typically, a customer stayed to see the finished product. Adding to the strangeness of the situation, I had not seen Austin. My son had gone home from school with his friend. He was inside. Somewhere.

I took measurements and prepped the aluminum siding to adhere the decals to the sides of the rusted van. As I worked, I thought it strange the boys had not come outside of the house when I arrived to greet me. This was uncharacteristic behavior as they were usually eager to say hello. What was different about today?

The van was positioned beside the house next to open windows. I could hear a man talking and a girl laughing. The more I heard giggling, the more anxious I became about Austin.

When I was nearly complete with the van, I sent a text to Austin. *Come out here and see me!*

A few minutes later, he came striding across the yard. One look at the dark circles under his red eyes and his uncharacteristic smirk, I felt a painful rush of parental anger, heartbreak, and disappointment.

"You're high." I gave him the *displeased mom look.*

His smile was immediately replaced with a look of anger and cockiness. "No, I'm not."

"Don't lie to me, Austin. I know what high looks like." I pointed toward our address. "You get your butt home. Now!"

I was so angry; I wasn't even thinking about the fact I had just told him to drive home while he was still high. I called his dad to let him know Austin was on his way home and he had been smoking pot with his buddy. Of course, that's why the customer left quickly after I arrived. He knew what was going on in his house, and he allowed it.

The first thing that came to mind was to nip this behavior in the bud right away. I wanted Austin to know there could be serious consequences if this continued. He was heading down a very serious path. Second, I wanted Mr. Father questioned about why my son and his were allowed to smoke an illegal substance in his home. Why was he not protecting our children?

Austin's dad and I both arrived at the jail at the same time. Austin got out of his dad's car wearing a nervous and disgruntled expression. My heart sank for him, but at the same time, I prayed this would be enough to scare him away from another episode of drugs. Hopefully, being questioned by an officer at the police station would keep my sixteen-year-old son from becoming involved in drugs.

This wasn't the only time their dad and I had taken the boys to the police station. The first time was when we found out David had been drinking with friends at a sleepover. These boys had met through one of the after-school programs. David was invited to spend the night. Later, I learned they slept in a tent in the backyard with no supervision at a grandfather's home. One of the boys brought alcohol.

After that sleepover event, their dad and I took both boys to the police station where the officer explained the consequences that could come if David drank alcohol again while underage. At age fourteen, David stood along the wall of the interrogation room with his hands together behind his back as tears streamed down his face. Austin stood beside his brother, watching and listening intently to what was being said. He displayed nervousness but also looked with sympathy at David as the officer clearly outlined the consequences of breaking the law.

But this visit to the police station was different. The officer interviewed Austin and asked all the standard questions. Who, what, when, where, and why. There was something about the officer's inquiries that felt to me like he was being dismissive about the situation. Didn't this police officer understand this behavior was scary? That if he continued, Austin could experience significant problems in his life? That this choice would have a huge and terrible impact on my family?

My kids didn't come from a home where drugs were the norm or okay. We were a Christian family. I had taken the necessary steps to provide for us to now live in a peaceful home where the kids knew they were loved. Our residence was a clean home, and they were well provided for. Drugs and alcohol were not acceptable in our little bubble of the world.

"You tell him the truth, Austin." I sternly encouraged my son. "It's always best to tell the truth."

Austin told the police the father let them smoke marijuana at his home. His friend's sister's boyfriend, a young man in his twenties, sold the drugs to Austin. The officer recognized the names Austin shared.

"I want to speak to the father." Looking at the opposite end of the table where the officer sat in his blue uniform with a shiny silver badge mounted on his chest I said, "I want to ask him personally why he would allow this in his home? Why would he not protect my son?"

"Ma'am, that would not be a good idea." The officer said they had already had many dealings with this guy. "He can get pretty heated, and it gets ugly. It would not be a good idea for you to approach him with this. I will talk to him and give you a call."

As we left the police station, I held hope the dealer would be dealt with along with the owner of the house.

The next day the officer telephoned. "I wanted to call and let you know I did drive over, and I spoke with the boy's father. He lets the kids smoke there because he feels if they are going to do it, at least they are safe there. I also questioned the kid who sold Austin the pot. He said he didn't know Austin wasn't eighteen yet."

What? I screamed inside. *Number one, Austin doesn't look anywhere near eighteen with his baby face. Second, since when is it legal to sell marijuana in Indiana to someone you think is eighteen?*

My anger boiled to realize there would be no consequences for these two adults who were doing illegal things and involving my minor son in illegal activities. Why was this officer so dismissive of a situation that was vitally important to me? Were there underlying reasons this policeman was not upholding the law?

Later, I learned David had also been given marijuana. That explained David's sudden newfound interest in going with Austin to this friend's house.

And so, the nightmare began.

CHAPTER FOURTEEN

Pounding Waves

David consistently made As and Bs academically in his school grades.

A good student, David had never been the subject of calls from the principal's office. Occasionally, a teacher told me he wasn't paying attention, but that was the extent of issues at school. However, in his tenth-grade year, David began getting in trouble at school. With new friends, he experimented with alcohol and pot.

One day, as David rode the bus home from school, his friend slapped him hard on the back of the head. David thought the slap came from another boy, and the next day, David slapped the kid back in retaliation. The kid explained he had not been the one to hit David.

The following day, word circulated the young man who David had struck was talking badly about David and the incident. David's friends conspired to jump the boy after school when he got off the bus at his bus stop. David and Austin went along with the plan and drove to the bus stop next to the boy's house in time for the husky teen to step off the school bus.

Jumping out of the car, David and his friend sprinted across the yard to fight the kid. David was not a fighter, so the punches he threw mostly hit air. The boy's grandmother saw what was happening through her living room window and called the police.

The next day at school, David and the kid passed each other in the hallway. The kid taunted David and made smart remarks. David retaliated by pushing the kid. A janitor stepped between the two before anything more happened.

A premeditated punch that never physically touched the boy, and a push resulted in battery charges for David. The incident seemed like a schoolyard brawl that might get a student sent to the principal's office for a lecture or maybe suspension back in my school days. However, David's actions resulted in a juvenile record. This would only be the first of my frustrations as a parent with the legal system.

Along with the battery charges came probation. When David was tested for drugs and alcohol, he tested positive for marijuana. Those first couple of nights in a youth facility began his journey in youth correctional facilities and youth residential homes.

In my journal, I wrote my prayer.

April 19, 2018

Life can sure get tough when the waves seem to pound against me all at one time.

The business has been incredibly busy the last two weeks filling large orders for ball leagues. Wonderful, but I'm working so many hours and my body is weary.

Customer payments have been delayed, vendors call wanting money, and our designer gave two weeks notice at this busiest time of the year.

In the midst of all this, I caught both boys smoking marijuana in the house again. David's court date is only one week away.

I sat them both down and told them, "I do not want my boys smoking pot or doing any other drugs. Your brains are still developing until you're 23 years old. Austin, if you're struggling with concentration, it's because of the pot. You need to stop. I do not want it in my house. I do not want it on my property. If someone walks in our house right now, they would smell it. I would go to jail! If I smell it again, I will not come to your room; I will not confront you about it. I will just call the police and they can bring their dogs and find it. You're old enough to make a choice and pay the consequences of those choices. If it happens again, don't plan on privacy in your bedrooms because I'm taking off your doors."

The following Monday, we went to court. David received nine months of probation instead of a year because the judge believed I saw potential in David, and he took my word for it. The judge scheduled random drug tests.

The pressure of everything was building up. I did not feel well. One of my favorite uncles passed away on Friday evening, and I needed to attend the visitation at the funeral home. I tried my best to suppress my emotions, because letting them surface would only make me feel worse.

The boys' father had retired and kept the boys after school for me until my workday ended. On this night, I picked up Austin and David from their dad's house around 9:00 p.m. after I attended the visitation for my uncle at the funeral home.

The boys had gone upstairs to their rooms. Suddenly I heard fists pounding against flesh. A fight had broken out between them and this sounded like a bad one. When the aggression didn't end quickly, I went to the bottom of the stairs to say something to break it up.

Before I could call up to them, the fight stopped. Austin and David had been getting into fist fights recently and some were pretty ugly. This was unusual for them, so I wasn't sure if the behavior was spurred by teen hormones, or if the pot they were smoking created agitation, or if the fighting was a result of a little of both.

One evening, I sat on the floral print living room sofa to relax from the day and turned on my favorite television series, *Criminal Minds.*

Around 9:30 p.m. David came down the stairs. "Goodnight, Mom." He leaned over and kissed me on the cheek. "I won't be back down tonight."

"Good night, honey." His sweet gesture warmed my heart. "Love you."

"Love you, too." He retreated to his room.

I continued entering vendor data and numbers until I smelled a horrible aroma filtering throughout the house.

I stopped my work and sniffed. *What is that smell?*

Then I realized. "You've got to be kidding," I spoke aloud. "He's smoking pot in the house."

A few days earlier, I smelled pot carried into the house on the boys' clothes. They had walked down the road to smoke, thinking they would get away with it if they weren't close to home. That day, I sat them down and calmly explained the next time I caught them smoking, I would call the police, and they would have to suffer the consequences. The use of alcohol and drugs, including pot, was not acceptable.

Of course, at the time I gave my ultimatum, both boys were high. Their responses included giggles as Austin stared at me from the couch with a grin from ear to ear. David sat on the floor listening but without a care in the world.

Having so recently told my boys if I caught them smoking again, I'd call the police, what should I do?

I felt I needed to stand my ground as a parent and do what I told them I'd do. Yet, calling the police to report my son was not what I really wanted to do.

"Lord," I prayed, "is this the right thing to do? I don't want them getting into trouble. Hopefully, the officer will just scare him a bit and put an end to all of this."

The officer arrived around 10:00 p.m. I paced the living room, praying I was doing the right thing until the headlights lit up the drive as the police car pulled down the lane.

Officer Jackson came to the front door and knocked. "You called the police department about your son."

"Yes." I felt relief when I recognized the officer as the son of another sheriff I knew who had worked with my father. As kids, we spent some time at his house. I hoped what was to come would go smoothly. If David could be made aware of what could happen if he continued smoking pot, perhaps he could be scared into doing what was right and legal. This tactic worked previously with his underage drinking so there was a chance the night would end peacefully.

"David is in his room." I climbed the stairs with the uniformed officer following closely behind. "I told him if I caught him smoking pot again, I would call the police."

Stopping in front of my son's bedroom door, the officer knocked. "David, open up. This is Officer Jackson."

There was a moment of silence before the door opened.

"Smells like pot in here, David." The officer motioned for David to come out. "Step outside the room and sit on the stairs."

Looking nervous and angry, David crossed the hallway in front of me and sat down on the second carpeted step.

The officer pulled out dresser drawers and dumped clothes into a heap on the floor. On the nightstand, the policeman found my son's cell phone and handed it to me. "You might want to hang on to that for a while. He doesn't need to be calling his dealers."

Holding the phone, I sat on the stairway landing one step behind David.

Next, I heard the policeman open the bedroom closet. The thud of boxes hit the back of the closet wall. Other boxes dropped to the floor as he continued his search. The air between David and me grew tense. The sound of hundreds of Legos spilled onto the carpet radiated into the hall. David was saving his childhood Lego collection for his own children one day.

"You might want to get rid of your toys, David." The officer called from the bedroom. "You want to mess with adult things? Time to grow up."

I felt sorry for David as his room was ransacked. The officer extended no mercy. David sat calmly on the hallway step in front of me, but I could see his complexion turning red as silent anger built.

"I found enough to charge him with possession of paraphernalia." Officer Jackson walked out of David's room carrying a homemade pipe. "I think he dumped what was left of the pot out onto the roof. Is he on probation?"

"Yes." My heart sank. The last thing I wanted for David was more charges on his record. *Lord, did I do the right thing?*

"I'll file the paperwork. You need to notify his probation officer in the morning." He made his way to the stairs. "David, you're going down the wrong path. I hope you get it figured out soon."

The officer left, and I went straight to my bedroom. David suddenly ran down the steps, and I knew what he was after. I ran through the master bathroom to the walk-in closet. Inside were twelve-by-twelve-inch clothing bins on wooden organizer shelves. I pulled one out and quickly hid David's cell phone under some garments.

When I turned around, there stood David behind me, trapping me between him and the basket where I had just hidden his phone.

"Mom." He looked at me with rage. "Give me my f@#k'n phone."

"You're not getting your phone back, David." I met his eyes which were full of desperate anger.

He lunged toward the shelves, rapidly rummaging through items he could quickly grasp. I sighed with relief when he retreated before searching the bin behind my head where the cell phone lay hidden.

He stepped back and shouted. "Give it to me, B!t@h!"

In one quick motion, I slapped him across the cheek. It took us both by surprise.

David balled up his fist, cocked his arm behind his head, and prepared to throw a hard punch. My heart broke for both of us. *How did we get here? How did my sweet Davie get to this place?*

His arm was frozen in time as he glared at me. Tears began to stream down his red cheeks.

Evenly, I spoke. "Really? Is this where you want it to go, David?"

"You hit me." He bit out the accusation.

"I told you," I reminded, "if you ever called me a name like that, you would get smacked."

"I just want my phone back." He returned to the initial demand. "Please give me my phone back."

"You're not getting it." I stood firm on my decision.

To my surprise, David turned and left the room without another word. I wasn't sure where his mind was, especially since he was still under the influence of the marijuana he smoked. Feeling an overwhelming uneasiness, I closed and locked the bedroom door.

I sat on the edge of my bed to take a moment to calm and collect my emotions. The silence was abruptly broken as the bedroom doorknob was twisted back and forth from the outside.

I watched the knob in anticipation of what would come.

Bam. Bam. Bam.

The insistence of his attack on the door startled me.

"Open the door, Mom," he yelled. "I want my F'n phone! Give me my phone."

Bam, bam, bam.

"And you need to get upstairs and clean my room." His demands escalated. "You caused this. I want my phone."

"I'm not cleaning your room, David." I waited to see if he was listening. "I told you what would happen if you brought drugs into my house again. I warned you. You will have to clean your own room."

The door vibrated from the force of his pounding.

"God, help us." Burying my face into a pillow, I prayed. "This is not him, Lord. David's a good kid with a compassionate heart, and normally, he is a joy to be around. What are these drugs doing to him? This is not my son. Please, help him. Please, help us."

I heard frustration on the other side of the door through his weakening voice. David's emotions welled to the point of childlike sobbing.

Slowing my breathing, I felt like we were in someone else's true story movie.

"I just want my phone, Mom." He cried in an exhausted retreat. I heard his hands slide down the door and pictured him with his forehead rested against the panel.

Then came silence.

I remained motionless on the bed for a while. The house grew quiet as the clock ticked into the early hours of the morning. I unlocked the door to my bedroom and slipped out to turn off the living room lights and lock the doors. I stopped at the refrigerator dispenser to fill my glass with ice and cold water.

The uneasiness of the situation hadn't left. I had never seen David act that way before. Had the pot he smoked been laced with something that carried behavioral side effects? What might he do next?

Back in my bedroom, I locked the door behind me. What a terrible feeling to lock myself behind closed doors because I felt afraid of the son I dearly loved.

Turning on the soft light next to the bed, I placed the fresh glass of water on a coaster on the nightstand beside my journal and my mother's Bible. In the bathroom, I went through my usual nighttime routine, put on my pajamas, and brushed my teeth.

When I opened the bathroom door, David rushed quickly from where he had been hiding in the back den. He was dressed in jeans and a black hoodie with the hood pulled over his head, concealing his hair.

Startled at his unexpected appearance, I screamed. "David! You scared me."

My heart pounded, as I realized I was now locked in the room *with* him. "What are you doing in here?"

David quickly reached for something on my nightstand. The glass clunked as it hit the table, toppled onto the carpet, and water spilled out.

I rushed over and unlocked the door anticipating I may need to flee. I now found myself cornered between David and the door.

"Move, Mom!" he said sternly as he attempted to leave the room. You need to give me my phone back. I've got yours!" He taunted as he held my mobile phone above his head and shook it as a tease. "What are you going to do about it, Mom? You can't call for help now."

Fear washed over me. David was right; I had no way of calling for help if he should do something horrible. I had never felt fear of my son before tonight. This situation had increased far beyond my initial hope that a taste of the consequences resulting from smoking marijuana would give David reason to reconsider his choices.

"I'm not giving you the phone, David." I went to the kitchen to get a towel.

Back in my bedroom, I picked up the empty drinking glass from the floor. Using the kitchen towel to clean up the water spilled on the nightstand, I noticed only a small puddle in a very confined area on the tabletop. Gingerly, I lifted my journal, expecting the book to be soaked and the pages ruined. Instead, the journal remained completely dry. Next, I lifted my mother's Bible, again certain the pages would be drenched by the spreading puddle. To my surprise, the Bible felt dry.

Where did all the water go? I looked behind the nightstand to see if the water had run down the back instead of the front of the table. I ran my hand down the cardboard backing and found only a cobweb and dust. No moisture. The furniture was bone dry.

David dropped down on the edge of my bed, shoulders slumped, and my phone held loosely in his lap.

I knelt near David and patted the carpet. The water had to have made something wet.

"What am I supposed to do, Mom?" David spoke calmly. "You caused this. You shouldn't have called the cops."

"David, I told both of you boys if you brought drugs into the house again, I was going to call the police." While I spoke, I felt the carpeted area around the nightstand. "You brought this on yourself."

The floor felt barely damp. *Where did the water go?* "David, did you drink some of my water?"

"What?" He squinted as if trying to follow my question while wrestling his own thoughts.

I repeated my question. "Did you drink some of my water?"

He answered with some sarcasm. "No."

David continued to chat about something, but my ears stopped hearing his words. I could see him talking but heard only muffled sounds.

"Even now," spoke a familiar voice, "I am protecting you."

I felt the peace of God come over me. I knew angels protected my journal and Bible. These two items would be important in the days ahead.

God was with me, protecting me, and watching over both of us. I could rest.

Later, I asked David, "Why didn't you hit me?"

He softly replied, "Because I knew I could never hit my mom."

CHAPTER FIFTEEN

Broken Anchor

After a trip together to Texas, Mark was invited to move there and work with his cousin in ministry.

The weekend we visited was wonderful, but I sensed what was about to happen. All I could do was cry. I knew he was going to take the offer.

This was a chance to start a fresh life and leave his heartbreak behind. I hoped I'd be enough to fill the hole for him, but he decided to accept the offer and not take me with him. I felt like half my soul was missing.

My mom came to visit, and I liked having her near to spend time with, but I could sit in a room of a thousand people and still feel completely alone. My heart had been shattered.

"I just can't find joy, Mom." I told her as we sat on the porch looking over the pond.

She looked up from her crossword search puzzle. "Well, Honey, you're grieving."

Grieving. I had not thought of it that way, but she was right. I had lost loved ones I was extremely close to, but never felt this deep of a pain. Once Mom returned home, I filled my empty hours with prayer and journaling. I constantly had televangelists on the TV or praise music playing. I searched for peace and understanding of what just happened and why.

"Why, Lord, after everything I had been through in my previous marriage, why would you put this man in my life, and take him away from me?"

Every step of the way God walked with me and gently showed me new things through the heartache. In this season came the lessons of the heart. The loneliest time of my life became the most precious time with my Jesus.

One morning, I lay in bed and heard a songbird outside my window. I smiled. "Thank you, Lord, for the sweet sound of the songbird that fills my heart with joy."

Every day after, I searched for anything in my day that brought joy. I had to look to see it, but I found joy in the laughter of my boys, a song on the radio, a cloud, a bird in the sky, a little old man holding his wife's hand.

With each moment that I remembered joy in the darkness, I thanked God for a small blessing. Little by little, over time, the darkness dissipated though the heartache remained for years to come.

CHAPTER SIXTEEN

God the Navigator

I spent time talking with God when the boys were with their dad. During my healing since Mark and I broke up, I was learning about God's ways. One evening, I asked God to confirm if it was time for me to step into my calling as a speaker, writer, and artist. Since childhood, I had a passion for helping the hurting and bringing them closer to Christ.

However, I only seemed to do what I felt were small things for the Lord. On my prayer wall, I posted, "Lord, use me as your instrument to reach thousands and not just a few." I had waited twenty-one years for bigger doors to open.

Years before, while I was married to my ex-husband, as I sat in the old tan recliner, the small lamp on the stand lit my small corner of the room. My laptop rested on my lap while I worked on T-shirt designs. On the television, Joyce Meyer taught.

"God," I asked, "what do you want me to call my ministry? *Your* ministry when it is time for me to step into it?"

In my spirit, I heard the words *Lessons of the Heart*. That title I had been given all those years ago aligned perfectly with what he was beginning to show me. The title aligned with the term I was given by the Lord years before.

Through my time seeking to comprehend and accept the loss of Mark, I related to people in the Holy Bible. Job, Abraham, and Sarah knew heartache. Their stories and life lessons connected with me in fresh ways.

Mark and I remained best friends and often texted. He asked if he could commission me to do an oil painting of Christ on the cross based on a vision he had. As I thought about the power of this image, I saw something more.

I imagined myself walking into a large hall or the gym of a church building. As I entered the hall, I was greeted by a patron who handed me a headset and pointed me toward a large painting set up like the backdrop of an exhibit booth. Polyester fabric stretched tautly between poles and gave the image a curved shape. Lights above illuminated the painting.

Ushered over to stand in the middle of the curve, I felt hugged by this life-size image. Through the headset, music played. Next, I heard my own voice telling the story of this image as the *lesson of the heart*.

When the story was told, I saw another painting and another and another. Each had been positioned, so I could weave in and out like winding through a show at an art gallery. At the end of these full-size portrayals, a magnificent surprise brought me to tears.

Through this vision, I understood God wanted me to use my gift of painting and the lessons he had taught me through the heartache I experienced. I could share the hope he gave to me with others to help them overcome their trials. Those stories would remind viewers there was a way to get through their circumstances. There was a *lesson of the heart* they would receive and hold on to forever.

That night, I sat on the bed and pondered what I had seen. "Please confirm for me this is a vision from you and not just my overactive imagination going wild. Was this you? Is this something you want me to do?"

I had recently listened to a sermon by Robert Morris on how to hear God, so I decided to write down my prayer as he suggested. "Through writing," he said, "God will lead you, and you will be surprised at how much you will hear and learn from God."

I took out my pen and journal and began to write.

May 20, 2018

Lord, is this Lessons of the Heart traveling painting show really from you? Is this my purpose?

For years, I have felt I would one day paint again and use my talent you gave to minister to others. But I didn't see a way to really make an impact. I'm not Thomas Kinkade nor will I ever be. But you have given me a wonderful gift.

When the ideas of the painting for Mark came up, I suddenly felt this was the answer. The show is not about beautiful landscapes that would reside in a home interior magazine, but symbolic of the lessons you are teaching me.

I can see how organizing events at church and through Crossroads has developed my abilities for an incredible journey of events across the US and maybe even beyond.

The event I did that stands out the most is the Fall Fest Bible Walk Through. Ushering hundreds of people through twelve scenes, settings, and stories. That experience prepared me for this.

Is this of you God, or my own creative mind setting me up for failure?

I have to believe this is from you by the way the enemy has hit me so hard trying with all his might to crush and take everything from me. My health has gotten worse, employees quitting or leaving, the financial struggle with the company, and my boys in serious trouble and outright rebellion. Personal property breaking down, family dying, and on and on. I am tired, overworked, and underpaid. There is not much energy or strength left in me without your intervention.

You have said in 1 Corinthians 10:13 ESV, "No temptation has overtaken you that is not common to man. God is faithful, and he will not let you be tempted beyond your ability, but with the temptation he will also provide the way of escape, that you may be able to endure it."

How much more will you allow to be oppressed upon me? Days have come that I felt I could barely move another step. The exhaustion is great, and my burden is so heavy I feel I could collapse under the weight. Joy is hard to find amongst the chaos. I long for my life to return to normal, but I don't see sight of it anywhere in the near future.

This has to be the enemy trying to snatch my health, finances, employees, relationships, loved ones, business, and children from me.

So Lord, this battle is because I am your Battle Axe, isn't it? A battle axe is a weapon of war. God, use me as your weapon against the enemy. The battle axe you have shown me through another dream. I have seen my purpose; to teardown strongholds through this show, writing, and speaking. This is how I will affect thousands as I have prayed to do for so many years. If I am wrong, please close this door. Let these images pass from me quickly.

When I wrote the word *strongholds*, I questioned my choice of words and remembered I had written something about strongholds back in the journal when researching the battle axe after having the other dream. I turned back to that reference and read. "A battle axe is a weapon in the hands of the warrior that can bring down the enemy. It has the capacity to cut down, root up, and break into pieces the strongholds of the enemy."

In that next moment, I felt an intense sensation in the pit of my stomach that traveled through my body and surfaced at the top of my head. The power of the moment caused goosebumps on my arms and the hair to stand up. When it reached the top of my head, I had to close my eyes for a moment because it was a like a head rush, that ended with an ultimate release. My interpretation was the Holy Spirit living inside expressed pleasure in my acceptance of my call by making himself known in my physical body. An immense feeling of joy came over me. All I could do was sit and laugh with my Savior.

Then I asked, "God, is now the time to walk into my calling? I've been waiting for years. Please confirm for me this was a vision from you and not just my imagination going wild. Was this you? Is this something you want me to do?"

The moment I stopped speaking, I heard a voice in my inner being so clearly it felt like the Lord was sitting next to me. "Valerie, if you do this and follow me in obedience, you may have to be willing to lose your dream home, your dream business, and one of your sons to drugs and alcohol."

I sat for a moment in silence. I had seen God work in my life. Through previous loss, abuse, and heartache, I knew I could trust him. Whatever reason He had for me to go through more, there would be a greater purpose. The sacrifice could be worth it if people came to know him. I had been waiting for twenty-one years for God to use me. I had written on my prayer wall, "Lord, use me to reach not just a few, but thousands. Use me as your instrument."

"Yes, Lord," I responded. "Whatever you need me to do."

CHAPTER SEVENTEEN

Praise in the Storm

June 25, 2018

"Lord, today is full of emotions. I don't know what I should feel right now. David was once again angry and rebellious, making a scene at the courthouse. No one trusts his ability to control this behavior. We don't know what to do with him. The judge doesn't know what to do with him. The news David must stay at a Juvenile Center for a month came as a blow. We weren't expecting it. In some ways, my heart breaks. In another way, my heart feels relief, knowing my son is safe and out of trouble. I didn't want this for him. I want my son to have the best chance possible for a good life. Please step in and change his direction. Show the best way to help him. My heart breaks for him."

On David's sixteenth birthday, he entered his first long-term stay at a juvenile center.

Despite the circumstances, I wanted to make David's birthday special for him. I called the director of the facility and asked if I could surprise him with a cake on our next Sunday family visit.

"We believe in family support," the director said. "I have no problem with you bringing a birthday cake."

In the cooler, I placed the birthday cake, napkins, and plates with pictures of balloons on them, along with plastic silverware and red plastic cups for drinks.

Bob, Austin, and I arrived at the facility still dressed in our church clothes. We entered the building, excitedly pulling our blue and white cooler on wheels. We signed the guest book at the front desk, and a middle-aged gentleman ushered us down a dimly lit hall to a visitation room. Inside, a long brown table and chairs were the only furniture that occupied the space. I emptied the cooler and arranged the table to look like a birthday party.

An attendant went to get David. We stood, waiting with anticipation. I held the camera, ready to capture his look of surprise. Soon, David entered through a side door.

"Surprise," we shouted together. "Happy birthday, David!"

Startled, David jumped back. Then a beaming smile crept across his face. The photo I took captured perfectly the moment of surprise. The joy I felt was reflected on the faces of the others. How long it had been since we felt this welcome emotion.

David opened his card and several small gifts. I set them aside to return home with us because he wouldn't be able to retain them at the residence. Next, we shuffled and dealt the tattered cards to the UNO game the facility had provided. Once the winners were declared and we were tired of playing cards, the three of us took turns arm wrestling with David. Faces red with intensity, and giggles in the heat of the moment, we shared much-needed belly laughs.

David was tall and slender; he had lost his tween husky physique. Though long and lean, that boy had an amazing amount of strength in his toned arms. He took first place, of course, in our wrestling competitions.

When we left, I savored the moments. It had been a great day. The four of us had celebrated David's birthday together, and David was in a safe place. That's all that mattered at that moment.

July 4, 2018

Lord, I am trying to understand these trials I face. The constant pounding of the waves, and the roar of the storm is so deafening I do not hear you.

My sixteen-year-old son has been taken from me and sits in juvenile detention. Whites Residential looms ahead for us. I have lost an employee due to theft, my designer to a better salary offer, and my printer due to her quick temper. To make matters worse, I found out my intern will not be working half days for me through the school program as we had thought. Another bombshell is my customer service employee has given two weeks' notice.

What is this God? What am I doing so wrong to cause all of this?

This employee said nothing had happened, nothing was wrong. He merely got a better offer. But you know how this appears and feels to me. Have I sinned in some way to cause this fall? Is this part of your plan for me? Did you not bless me with the greatest year of my life when you gave me Mark and this company? Is it really you who gave me this, but now you're taking it away?

Is it as Job has said, "Naked I come from my mother's womb, and naked I will depart. The Lord gave and the Lord has taken away; may the name of the Lord be praised," Job 1:21 (NIV).

It was said, "In all this, Job did not sin by charging God with wrongdoing," verse 22. Job praised you even in his loss.

Is it you who is allowing this, Lord? Would you incite Satan against me to ruin me without reason? I continue to trust you, Lord, even in all of this! My health has declined, so I cannot do what I used to do. Through the loss of the man I thought I was to marry.

Through the loss of my son to rebellion and drugs. Through loss of financial stability and loss of employees. Through the possibility I may lose my company and then my beloved piece of heaven... my home.

Through my Job experience, I still trust you have my best interest in mind; trust you love me. I seek and request your leading. Am I not keeping with my integrity?

"Satan can only go to the end of his chain," John Newton said. So how much more, Lord? How long is his chain? He may be exhausting me, discouraging me, and making me question your involvement. But God, I will not stop trusting you or curse you. I don't know what I would do without you in my life. Do I go to the left or to the right? I wouldn't know. I do not know how to not praise you. You've been in my life deeply since I was a young girl.

Lord, I do question, are you moving these employees out to allow me to start over and be successful, or is this Satan trying to crush me? I can't imagine you would take my designer at the busiest time of the year for me and cause me all that stress. I do believe you tried to bring his replacement when you brought the intern.

Why have you not brought me a printer, Lord? Though you helped me take the brunt off my plate by providing Jose part-time. But Lord, you know I cannot physically handle the heat or physical stress of printing. I feel I'm being forced into contract printing and by bringing me no one, I will have no choice.

But how do we transition with so much debt? I can't pay the bills. I know you would not want me to file bankruptcy. There has to be another way. A way to keep my integrity.

God, I know you brought my friend, Heather, to help. Why bring Heather, though, just to shut down the business and put her out of a job? Unless to prepare her for a better one?

The day before my designer gave his notice and then again when the customer service rep gave his, I was at home sick and resting. I hadn't stayed home like that in a long time. I believe both those days were to prepare me to handle this news. You were protecting and preparing me. I know your hand is in this, but why not bring me a printer? Why these constant attacks? You always brought my ex-husband an employee to fill empty positions. Why not me? Do you want this to fail. And why would you? Unless for a greater purpose?

I felt when all this trouble started I may have to lose everything to be a greater testimony. Please lead, God!

Lead me… I pray! Give me strength through each trial. Teach me how to respond. Help me to praise you through the storms and prepare me to be a testimony. Thousands, Lord! I want to help thousands! Prosper me and my children. Turn their hearts toward you and let us serve you as a family. Give me a gentle spirit. The voice of the proverbial woman. The faith of a Godly woman. Restore my weak faith to the rock it once was. I don't know whether to go to the left or to the right without you.

The only word you have given me is, Simplify. What exactly does that mean? We have lost $50K in the first six months of this year compared to last year's first six months. Why?

God, I do believe painting and writing about these lessons is my future purpose. I'm anxious to get started. But I am trapped. I want to have integrity. You have not said to sell or to close. But how do we make it? And how am I to prepare this material when my time is spent feeling ill, exhausted, or solving business problems?

You have provided for me, yet this company eats away at what I have. I have a short time for funds to be available so that I do not have to work. Please don't let Satan keep me from proceeding.

CHAPTER EIGHTEEN

Rain Sorrows

D avid lived at Paddock View Youth Residential for a month, but that short time changed our lives forever.

He met a kind, young woman there who he felt comfortable being with. The lady was assigned to monitor his health and vitals because the pot he had smoked caused his blood pressure to climb sky-high. His openness with her gave us hope because sharing his inner thoughts and feelings had been challenging for him. She kept me up to date on how he was doing and his current mindset. She seemed to be a positive influence.

When David was released, I called the young woman and asked if she would mind staying in contact because she was the only one he seemed to listen to. I wanted him to have someone he could confide in. She agreed and was pleasant when she was around our family. David confided in her, and she began confiding in me as a mother figure. I enjoyed being a mentor for her.

Before long, it became apparent David and the young woman had developed a relationship beyond mentoring. David was sixteen. She was older, but her maturity and appearance didn't fit her age. David's behavior settled, and he seemed to be making better choices.

His dad and I hoped she was the answer to helping him turn his life around.

David's father and I met when I was eighteen. There were twenty-five years between us when we married, and both of us were keenly aware trying to come between them could lead to more rebellion. My family had not been in favor of our marriage, leading to a lot of hurt, unacceptance, and distant relationships for a while. I didn't want to repeat that scenario with my kids, so we chose not to discourage their relationship.

Instead, I gave my concerns to God in prayer. I was confident God knew best, and he'd have to be the one to intervene. Not everyone viewed the situation that way, and we found ourselves with a bigger battle to fight in the days to come.

During this period of time, over the course of a week, I dreamed about my ex-husband. I hadn't seen or talked to him in a while, so I didn't understand what was triggering the dreams. The dream I had on Wednesday morning wouldn't leave my memory.

In this dream, we attended a gathering of people with his family and friends. I felt anxious because I wasn't sure if it was acceptable for me to be present or not.

He treated me with love and kindness, telling people, "It's okay, I want her here." What spoke volumes to me was his son and daughter-in-law were kind to me.

When I woke, I wondered why I was having these dreams. I sent a text to his sister, told her about the dreams, and asked how he was doing. She gave an update, explaining he was currently in a nursing home and progressing very slowly. He couldn't walk on his own, talk much, or use his hands well.

The following Tuesday my cell phone rang. I saw his sister's name on the caller identification and instantly felt a knot in my stomach.

"I didn't want to call you at work," his sister began, "but I didn't want to wait and have you hear it another way."

Tears sprang to my eyes.

"He's gone," she said. "I know you love him. I wanted to be the one to tell you."

"Yes, I do," I choked out around the sudden lump in my throat. "Thank you. And I'm sorry." The call ended with a whispered goodbye through tears.

Silence filled the air as employees sensed the call had held bad news. My friend and bookkeeper, Heather, came and wrapped her arms around my neck. She held me tight as the sobs erupted and tears fell to the desk in front of me.

God, I never got to say goodbye. I had prayed when it was time, he would ask for me. Instead, there was no shared last laugh, no holding his hand as he entered glory, no last goodbye.

Many times, I had thought about going to visit, especially after the dreams started. But when I asked God if I should go, I heard, "No, he doesn't want you to see him this way." For his sake, I felt led to stay away.

After the call, I understood the meaning of the dream. For the two years he had been sick, my question had been, when he passed should I go to the funeral? Through the dream, God prepared my heart and let me know it was okay to go to the funeral because he would have wanted me there.

Nervous, I walked into the funeral home wondering what to expect from the family or even myself. I had already texted his sister to ask if she felt it was acceptable for me to attend, and she encouraged me to come at the appointed time.

What I didn't expect were the emotions I felt when I stepped into the hall where he lay. His sister-in-law, one of my favorite people in the family, and his cousin greeted me at the entrance. I didn't expect the wave of sadness and loss to hit my heart so hard. My heart ached as if I were still married to him and no time had been lost.

His sister-in-law hugged me.

"I don't know if I can do this," I told her tearfully.

"Yes, you can." Her voice was strong. "Do you want us to go with you?"

Her support brought welcomed relief. His cousin hugged me.

I worked to pull myself together as we walked through the mingling family and friends.

His aunt and her daughter jumped from their chairs and grabbed me in an embrace. "The memorial you posted on social media was so beautiful. Just beautiful."

> My dearest,
>
> How we grieve today at the loss of your presence from us. When you fell ill, I questioned God and his timing and purpose. Why did he not let me know sooner? I knew the battle you faced before the day we sat on the porch, and you told me the news. I had already begun praying if you had to be hospitalized, God would grant me the chance to be by your side and care for you despite our circumstances. For your family to accept and embrace my help. Mere months later, I got the call, and God allowed me that blessing.
>
> It was an honor to care for you though a challenge for all at times. I thank your family for embracing that season for us, no matter how crazy it seemed. Circumstances changed, and the moment was shorter than expected, yet I hope you know how much I continued to love you behind the scenes.
>
> Our lives changed. We didn't make it through the trials of life together as planned, but no one can say our love wasn't genuine or deep. It never ended for either of us despite the obstacles we were handed.
>
> My heart grieves I never got that last laugh with you or to hold your hand at your last breath or the chance to say one last goodbye. But I know you knew my love remained, and you will always occupy a piece of my heart.
>
> Three years ago, you told me all you wanted was to go home to be with your daddy. It's been a long tough journey, honey, but today he welcomed you with open arms and a broad

smile. Your faith ran deep, you were strong, and you fought the good fight.

Now rest, my love, and enjoy that cattle ranch you dreamed of for so long. You made it! I'll see you on the other side. I'm sure he had a banner made just for you saying, *Rando's Chicken*. Make sure you have the BBQ chicken ready when I arrive.

His sister-in-law, cousin, and I continued to the front, and I felt the love radiate from the family who chose to surround me—the ex-wife. I felt grateful for his sister's embrace as we stood together at the casket and received what little amount of closure I could get.

The family was kind to me just like in the dream. God had spoken to allow me to know the man I still loved wanted me there.

CHAPTER NINETEEN

Rays of Sunlight

One evening, I got *the* phone call. The call no mother wants to receive about her sixteen-year-old son.

"Hi, Mom." I recognized the voice of the young woman David was in a relationship with. *Mom* was always a welcoming name from any friends of my boys.

"Hi there." I stopped in the middle of the living room, open to hear what she was calling about.

"David wanted me to call." She sounded nervous. "We have something important to tell you."

"Okay." My stomach tightened into knots, already anticipating her next words.

"I'm pregnant," she proclaimed boldly.

I tried to decide how to respond with love, and not show complete disappointment. At her age, why in the world wasn't she taking birth control pills? Surely, she was aware this could happen. Surely, he was aware, too.

"You are, huh?"

"David wanted me to tell you. He was too afraid. Yeah, we are." Her words were matter of fact. "I took the test, and it was positive."

"Well, congratulations! Children are a blessing, and I'm sure you're going to make a great mother. I'm glad you're mature enough and financially stable to take care of a child." I tried to sound encouraging and not let condemnation seep through my tone.

"We'll be fine," she said confidently. "I'll help David through this."

"Please include me in your appointments and things if you would. I look forward to being a grandma," I admitted. "Congratulations again. Keep me up to date on everything."

"Okay, I will," she agreed. Then we both said our goodbyes.

I sat on the edge of the couch, my phone still in my hand, and let out a big sigh. "God, this is not the way I pictured it for our family. A child out of wedlock. And David is only sixteen. Please help us through this. Please, let this be the turning point for David. Maybe you've allowed this baby to save David from himself."

Again, I had a choice to make. I could be angry and make the situation worse. Or I could look at it as a sign of hope and pray God worked everything out for our best. From that moment forward, I chose to embrace this child as a gift from God like every child is, despite the circumstances. We don't always choose how life will play out or make our child's decisions for them. I chose joy over sadness or anger and disappointment. I chose to love the baby. I chose to love them.

The fun and excitement began to build. I couldn't wait to be a grandma. I hoped this child would help David find a greater purpose and move him away from drugs. This child became the bright spot in my life. I couldn't wait to meet her.

CHAPTER TWENTY

Voyage Calling

*W*hat is Wycliffe?

I had never heard the word and now I was curious. I had just woken from another of what I call my spiritual dreams. They have a different feel to them than my average nighttime dream.

This one was incredibly specific.

I had been deeply questioning things happening in my life and praying God would guide me to what I should do. In the dream, I was at a friend's house following an evening out for supper. While my friend spoke to another guest, I found the restroom. Going in, I recognized I stood in my aunt's bathroom. When I was a child, I got off the bus at her house and spent a lot of time in her home.

In my dream, a woman appeared to be hanging a curtain at the far end of the room. At first, I thought she was a younger version of my grandmother. But the longer I stared, I recognized her as a younger version of my aunt.

I felt a presence behind me and turned to find a young woman in her thirties.

"I don't know what to do," I said to the woman near me.

"You are not to lose hope," she answered. "This is a process."

"What do I do?"

"We want you to wait." She led me toward the end of the room where the first woman worked and helped with whatever she was hanging.

I watched them as they were busy with their task. "How long?"

"Some details are better left unsaid," she replied. "We wanted to put you at Wycliffe, but it didn't work out." She stated with frustration in her tone.

Before I could ask more, I felt the presence of a very large being to my right. Though I couldn't see him, he stomped his foot with a thunderous boom. At that very moment, my alarm clock went off waking me. It was 7:30 a.m., and I knew I had been in the presence of God's messengers and a large and powerful angel.

I typed Wycliffe into my phone's online search bar. *Wycliffe Bible Translation* appeared.

"That can't be it," I said to myself. "I know nothing about Bible translation."

I sent a text to Mark. "Have you heard of the word Wycliffe?"

"I don't think so," he typed back.

"Can you ask your cousin if there is a Wycliffe town or city in Texas?"

Mark had recently moved into his cousin's home to do co-laboring work for his ministry.

"He says not that he knows of. There is a Wycliffe exit or street somewhere."

Searching the internet again, once again, it pulled up Wycliffe Bible Translation and listed their main office in Dallas, Texas where Mark had just moved.

I recalled an announcement our pastor made at the end of church service the morning before. "John is going to be teaching… Bible translation… See him to sign up."

I decided to phone John.

"Hi John, can you tell me what it is you are doing with this Bible translation thing?"

"Oh, you mean the banquet?" He asked.

"Ugh! No, not a banquet." I thought.

"We're raising money for Bible translation." He gave the details. "I can get you a ticket if you'd like to join us."

"Let me get back to you on that," I replied brushing it off with disinterest. "John, does the term Wycliffe mean anything to you?"

The line grew quiet.

"Well, yes, that is who this banquet is for," he said. "We are raising money for Wycliffe Associates who teaches Bible translators the techniques and provides tools and resources for people around the world to translate the Bible into their own language."

I paced the floor as I listened. "John, I don't know what you think of dreams or angels, but I dreamed an angel told me they wanted to put me at Wycliffe, but it didn't work out. And she seemed very frustrated about that."

There was another moment of silence. "I suggest you come to the banquet and find out what they are all about." He replied.

"I'll take a ticket." Then I recalled the dream I had had two years earlier. "Do they do anything regarding providing food?"

"Not unless you mean eating at the banquet." John laughed.

I was intrigued by where God was leading. At home that night, I sorted through the recyclables for yesterday's church bulletin. On the back was a photo of an old woman in colorful garb and the words Banquet Invitation.

Is this what the messenger of God wanted me to see, and I dismissed it because it was a banquet? Is that why the woman in my dream was frustrated?

Four days later, I prayed on the way to the Wycliffe Banquet. "God, I am open to whatever you want for me. If the name Wycliffe appeared in this dream only to confirm the first portion of the dream was from you, then that will be enough. If giving a donation is your reason for me to go, then that is enough. But if there is more for me to do, then I am available."

I recalled a friend's words, "Don't have expectations; but watch for God expectantly!"

The evening started with a well-prepared meal and a time to visit with John's family and another couple from our church. A video followed, depicting a young man seeking something in his life. He fell to the ground in a struggle, died, and was covered by the sand of the desert.

The videos played in three stages as the facilitator interjected explanations and stories. The third set of videos showed the images of dying people from my dream two years ago. There was death in the camp, starving people, and an evil presence.

God revealed I was to go and help feed them with spiritual food—the bread of life. Not a physical food as I had originally thought. A food that would raise them out of a spiritual death. Now I understood Wycliffe's mission. "The power of God's translated Word is bringing dead and dry souls new life."

I could take part in the great commission by going and providing equipment and training to help those in another country write the gospel in a language they could understand and give to their people.

The lights came up and we stood. John's wife approached. "What did you think?"

"I think God has work for me to do." If I said anything more, I would become a puddle of tears with a woman who knew little about me.

The same Sunday the pastor mentioned in his sermon, "You never know when God may call you to go to Africa."

"Well, that isn't going to be me," I said to myself. "I have no interest in going outside of the country. Especially to Africa."

Back home after the banquet, I wanted to laugh, cry, dance around the room in worship, and get on my knees in reverence. I felt joy, excitement, shock, fear, awe, and unworthiness, but at the same time, blessed.

Sunday, I had lunch with John and his family. They shared more about Wycliffe Associates, what they do, how their work affected people, and his part in it. I was eager to get involved with Wycliffe.

"I can't believe the great lengths God took to get you to talk to me!" John laughed.

"We're anxious to see how this turns out," John's wife said, "and how God uses you."

CHAPTER TWENTY-ONE

Warning!

The time was late when David went to his room to listen to his music and play on his phone.

In the den, I worked out on my weight machine until I heard a strange noise in the other room. When I went to investigate, everything appeared fine, initially. Leaning on the black granite counter, I peered around the kitchen and into the living room. Then I saw it.

For Christmas, one year I asked for a beautiful five-piece painting of the Lord's Supper. The rendition seemed to be a more accurate depiction of what it would have been like on that night around the table with Jesus. In this painting, the disciples sat on the floor, intently listening to the Lord speak.

The five panels hung on the living room wall centered above the floral-print loveseat. With the rich hues of browns, oranges, yellows, and dusty blues, the portrayal of such a significant moment in time brought warmth to the room.

Except the center panel now lay face down on the loveseat.

Strange. That painting has hung there for a year without incident.

Words echoed in my mind. *Where's your Jesus now?* I felt the enemy had just sent a message, mocking me and my Jesus.

Inspecting the back of the painting, I noted the Velcro that held the canvas to the wall was tightly attached to the wood strip of the canvas and to the wall.

"That's weird," I murmured aloud. "There is no reason for this to fall." I clicked the Velcro on the painting back into its center position of the pentaptych.

I turned off the living room light, locked the back door to the garage, and refilled my glass of water. It was approaching 11:00 p.m., and I was ready to go to sleep for the night.

Thud!

The sound woke me, and I lay in half a daze, trying to figure out what had just happened. The noise came from directly above my room as if Austin had dropped something heavy on the floor of his second-story bedroom. But Austin wasn't home tonight. A glance at the clock showed the time to be 11:30 p.m., an odd hour for David to be messing around.

I threw back the covers and went upstairs to see if for some reason David was in Austin's bedroom.

David's door was closed and the lights off; he was sound asleep. In Austin's room, I flipped on the overhead light. Squinting to adjust my eyes to the brightness, I expected to find something had fallen in the middle of the floor. But everything was in its place, and the only thing on the floor was a set of white speakers next to his bed that he liked to connect to his phone for the music he listened to.

"Austin isn't here. David is asleep," I mentally listed. "There is nothing in here that could have made that noise. Weird."

I went back downstairs, climbed into bed, and quickly fell asleep.

At 3:30 a.m., I awoke again. This time, I heard the sound of two people running through my kitchen and the doorknob to the garage turning. I jumped up and flung open the bedroom door, expecting to catch David trying to sneak out. It had happened before. This time I had him.

With the door wide open, I was ready to belt out my lecture but stopped in mid-breath when I realized no one was there. In the kitchen, the inside garage door remained locked. There was no sign anyone had run through the kitchen, unlocked the door, and relocked it as they went out. I opened the door to the quiet darkness of the garage. Turning on the light, there was nothing to see except my parked car.

I climbed the stairs again and checked on David. Once more, the room was perfectly quiet and dark as he slept. Back downstairs, I rounded the corner and found the centerpiece of the Christ painting face down once more on the loveseat.

I turned on the overhead lights and stood on the couch to inspect the Velcro strip that secured the art in place. The strip remained tightly adhered to the wall. The strip on the back of the painting was also tight. Confused, I rehung the panel to its original position, completing the five-piece image.

"Okay, God. What in the world is going on?" I spoke aloud. "I clearly heard someone running through my kitchen, but no one was there. There was a thud in Austin's room, too loud to deny, but he's not home and David is sound asleep. And now this Christ painting is pulled off the wall and lying face down for a second time. What is this about, Lord?"

I had studied about angels and demons and believed in their existence, knowing they both walk among us. Scripture described a constant unseen spiritual battle over us in the heavens.

"Which one is trying to send me a message," I asked. "Angels? Or demons? And why?"

The next day, around noon, I got a call from the school saying Austin had missed class periods one through four. I texted Bob to tell him Austin must have skipped school.

Not long after, Bob texted, "I just got a call from Austin in the Huntington County Jail. I'm in a restaurant and couldn't hear what he said."

"I'll call the jail," I replied, "and find out what's going on."

Because I was at work, I went into the bathroom for privacy and made the call.

My heart pounded as I asked the person who answered, "Do you happen to have my son, Austin, there?"

I silently prayed the response would be "No."

"Yes," The woman answered on the other end. "He was brought in last night and charged with possession of alcohol, trespassing, and mischievous conduct. They were breaking into a church."

Tears sprung to my eyes.

"His court date is scheduled, and bond has been set for $14,000," she continued. "You could call later to see if the judge lowers it."

The 26th. His court date was on the calendar for the 26th. *He won't be home for Christmas.* I didn't have the money for bail even if the amount was lowered. My son would spend Christmas in jail.

As I ended the call, my throat tightened, and tears streamed down my cheeks. I had to pull myself together before being seen by my employees. But all I could do was cry at the thought my son was going to be in jail over Christmas.

I called my dad and told him what I had just found out. Later, my dad called back and said they wanted to post the bail for Austin. Like me, his grandma couldn't stand the thought of him spending Christmas locked up. I felt relieved and grateful for their generosity.

CHAPTER TWENTY-TWO

Storm Sirens

Austin related to me the events of the previous night that ended in him being arrested.

Austin

My friend and I had gotten drunk on Candy Cane Smirnoff another friend had bought for us.

We were at my friend's girlfriend's house, and around 11:00 p.m., we ran out of alcohol and decided to walk to Walmart and get some more. We were both underage, so my friend planned to slip a bottle into his coat.

On the way there, we passed a church daycare. "Hey." He elbowed me in the ribs. "Let's break into this daycare and get some s$%t."

I don't remember much of what was said, because I was drunk, too. I just followed him to the door. He pulled a plastic credit card from his wallet and tried to get the lock to the building to release.

I watched him work the lock for a while but grew anxious. I didn't want to be involved in breaking and entering.

"F… this," I said and took off walking down the street. I hadn't gone far when I decided to go back to get him. That was a big mistake.

When I got back to the daycare, someone from across the street started yelling. Heart racing, I ran with my friend as we darted through the backyard of the church grounds and across neighboring yards. Thinking we were far enough away to avoid suspicion, we crossed back onto the sidewalk under the streetlights and walked back to his girlfriend's house.

A police cruiser pulled up along the curb and made us stop. Someone, maybe the guy who had yelled, had called and reported us. The officers took me to the police annex where they questioned me. I was arrested and charged with possession of alcohol, trespassing, and mischievous conduct.

My friend got to go home with his dad.

That evening, I remained at the shop after everyone else had gone home for the day.

The closed sign to the shop was turned, and the lights to the storefront were switched off. I remained in my office working on orders that had come in. Though my heart felt heavy, I focused my eyes on my computer. Soft music played in the background.

I heard the front door open and saw the dark silhouette of my dad in his hat and winter work coat. Austin meekly trailed behind him.

This was Austin's first experience in a jail; my little family's first experience with jail. Austin looked at me. I extended my arms to him.

Is this what the father felt like in the story of the prodigal son?

In that moment, I had a small taste of what God may feel when a child returns to him after leaving for a period and doing something to miss the mark. Jesus loves each son and daughter enough to extend grace and mercy.

We embraced, and Austin hugged me tight for an extended period of time. I didn't think he was going to let go. Dad watched from a distance in silence. All three of us had tears streaming down our cheeks.

Austin was home in time for Christmas. I hoped this would be a close enough call that Austin would choose to never go down this path again. I never wanted to have to feel *this* moment again.

Christmas evening, we gathered at my parents' home. When the meal was over and wrapping paper lay strewn across the living room floor, I sat at the end of my parents' couch, talking with a family member who sat next to me in my grandma's old swivel rocker.

"I think," he said, "we have ghosts in our house."

I nodded knowingly. "So do I."

I shared about the thud in Austin's room, the feet running through my kitchen, and my Jesus painting lying face down on the couch.

My family member described one late night when he was alone in the house. A thud sounded between the wall in the living room where he sat and his bedroom. The noise was so loud he thought someone had broken into his house through the window.

Checking his bedroom, there was no indication of what could have caused such a disturbing noise.

"The night I heard the mysterious sounds in my home was the same night Austin was drunk with his friend and they attempted to break into the church," I told him. "I wonder if *they* were trying to warn me about what Austin was doing. Or maybe they were mocking me."

"That's the same night I heard the sound in my house," he said. He agreed the sound was a warning about what Austin was doing.

I replayed the events in my mind. I wasn't the only one being sent a message. *I wasn't so crazy after all.*

CHAPTER TWENTY-THREE

Turbulent Waves

Stress compounded and weighed heavily as drug or alcohol charges multiplied and courtroom days increased. For months, I regretted weekends because each one brought a new phone call from the police or a new problem with either boy and sometimes both.

Would this horrible cycle ever end? Getting drunk or high was David's sole priority, and his grades plummeted from A and Bs to Ds and Fs. He became angry, moody, and difficult to be around. Peace disappeared, replaced by constant exhaustion and worry.

Adding to the overwhelming situation, David's probation officer acted unpredictably. Sometimes I felt he was an advocate, a safe place to talk about what was happening in my home because he had my son's best interest in mind. Depending on the day, he would be kind, comforting, and offer guidance.

The next day in court, he presented me as a terrible parent in front of the judge and caused additional charges to be added to David's already thick juvenile file. No matter how I handled the situation, I felt like we couldn't win.

I wanted help for my lost child. I needed a system that would come alongside me as a parent with guidance, encouragement, and support in my efforts to do what was best for David. Probation officers were trained to know what to do with kids that were belligerent, high, and out of control from substance abuse.

Feeling alone and scared, I was too aware of how little I knew about what to do to help my son. As a middle-class Christian family, I had raised my children in church, youth group, and in a loving home. We sat at the supper table as a family each night instead of in front of the TV. We took family vacations and spent quality time together. I attended the boys' sporting events, parent-teacher conferences, and was there for them no matter what. It came to a point I felt alone, ashamed, and determined to hide this dirty little family secret or be judged because my kids chose the wrong path. It had to be the parents' fault, right?

The source of joy I held on to was the coming baby. I couldn't wait to be a grandma. David was beginning to accept fatherhood and eagerly awaited the day he would see his firstborn. He looked forward to this baby.

On the day of the scheduled ultrasound, David and his special lady went in to share their moment together, while his grandma and I waited in the lobby. They were so cute sitting beside each other in the waiting room, hand in hand. We took photos of them to capture this moment. When she was called for her appointment, we watched them disappear down the hall together. I couldn't wait to meet this new person who brought into our family the joy and hope we desperately needed.

David's girlfriend shared she lost a child to a heart defect several years earlier, so we weren't completely surprised when she said this baby had heart complications. She invited me to accompany her to her obstetric appointment, but she didn't want me to go into the exam room with her to see the doctor. I sat in the lobby and waited for the news.

Before long, she developed miscarriage scares that required trips to the hospital. David was on house arrest and unable to go to the hospital the first night there was a crisis. During his next court session with the judge, we asked the court to grant David permission to attend doctor appointments or emergency hospital visits for the child, taking into consideration the baby's condition. This request was granted until…

Being honest and telling the truth was always a big deal to me, and I encouraged both of my sons to do the same. Even if telling the truth meant getting into trouble; not telling the truth held bigger consequences. In time, the truth became I could trust no one and silence was my best friend.

The system failed my family, and I felt like we were the victims of a very messed up process. My sons and I were put on trial as a family and individually. This realization came the day I was approached by his counselor in the courthouse hallway.

David's charges included mandatory counseling sessions at the Bowen Center. His counselor had recently questioned David about his girlfriend and the baby.

"Are you aware," the counselor said to me, "David's pregnant girlfriend is over the age of eighteen?"

"Yes," I replied. "I am aware she is over eighteen."

"Their relationship is against the law," she stated. "Are you going to press charges against her?"

"David's dad and I are not happy about the situation," I said, "but we had twenty-five years between our ages when we married. We know what happens when adults try to come between a couple's relationship. She seems to be good for David. We've seen a change in some of his decision-making. We are making the best of the situation and praying God intervenes where and if necessary."

On the next court date, I felt the pressure of being on trial myself as the prosecutor approached the judge's bench.

"That's the one that…" was all I heard as the prosecutor whispered to the judge. Based on my recent conversation in the hall with David's counselor, I was certain the prosecutor was making sure the judge knew I was the mother who was not prosecuting this young woman who carried my son's child. It appeared the counselors, probation officer, prosecutor, and the judge believed I was a failure of a mother for not protecting my son from her.

When Bob and I had talked over the situation, we concluded no good would come from prosecuting David's girlfriend. We didn't know everything about her, nor what was to come in the days ahead. We did know she was young lady that was pregnant with our grandchild and there appeared to be some maturity issues for her age. How would putting her in jail be helpful for her or David? And what would come of the baby?

Unsatisfied with our decision, the courts issued a restraining order. She was no longer allowed to see David.

With the news of the restraining order, the girl panicked. She claimed there was no baby, which caused an upheaval of emotions and uncertainty.

"Why," I asked, "would you lie about something like that?"

Her reasoning reflected her immaturity. "When they issued the restraining order, I got scared of going to jail. I thought, if there is no baby, the trouble would go away."

On the evening of January 4, I was lying on the loveseat and watching a movie when my phone pinged. Her roommate sent a text asking for prayer and requesting I tell David his girlfriend had been in a serious car wreck. She was being taken to the hospital.

The text included footage of the scene of the accident. The video wasn't good quality, but I could see the car and the lights from the ambulance and hear the siren blare.

That weekend, David was at his dad's house, so I called to tell him the news. His voice was somber with concern as we ended our conversation. David and I were reliant on her roommate to keep us up to date because David was on house arrest and couldn't go to the hospital.

I fell to my knees in the middle of the dimly lit living room. "God, I plead with you to hear my cry. Please protect this child and her mother. Be with the doctors and nurses and guide their hands. Give them the wisdom and the knowledge to know what to do and how to care for her. Bring complete healing over her, Lord. Comfort David and help him be strong. Wrap your arms around them all and lift our fear. We trust you, Lord. Thank you in advance for whatever you may do. Satan, you have no power or authority over her or her developing baby, and you must flee from them. God, please help! In Jesus name, Amen."

Ping. I read the new text.

"Please pray! They say she has a brain bleed, and there is only a sixty percent chance both her and the baby will make it."

The texts continued back and forth for another hour.

"If you had to make a choice," the words appeared on the phone screen, "would you spare her or the child?"

"Why are you asking me?" This was a bizarre question. "Isn't her family there to make that decision?"

"I'm here with her, but I can't make that decision. She is closer to you than her mom. She'd want you to make that decision."

I typed back. "Her!"

"Ask David what he wants. The nurse wants to know because he is the father."

Stunned, I didn't respond right away.

"Hurry, they need to know."

"David is at his dad's," I responded.

"Please go there now and ask him what he wants to do. Hurry! They need to know!"

Questions swirled in my mind. How could this be? Why David? Would medical staff really ask David to make this decision?

I drove to Bob's. As I pulled into the drive, a sick feeling gripped my stomach. I was about to walk in and ask my sixteen-year-old boy to choose between his baby and the woman he loved. "God help!"

In his bedroom, David sat in his recliner staring blankly at the movie on the television screen. The Christmas lights strung around the top of the room didn't feel so comforting right now.

"David, things aren't looking good." I couldn't believe these words were coming out of my mouth. "Her roommate texted and said the hospital wants to know, if they have to choose between the baby and her, what do you want them to do?"

This strange scenario felt like a movie playing in slow motion. But *nothing* was happening slowly; that was part of the problem. All I could do was react and process later.

He stared at the TV, yet I sensed his anger. "Her."

Concerned, I pressed. "Are you going to be okay?"

"Please just leave." His eyes stayed fixed on the screen.

I left with a heavy heart. No sixteen-year-old should make these kinds of decisions. He should be watching movies with his friends and eating pizza without a care in the world outside of graduating high school.

I returned to the car and texted David's response to the roommate. It was getting late, and the updates stopped for the rest of the night.

In the morning, I texted her roommate to check on them. The report came back she and the baby were going to be fine. I finally got to text her personally. The bleed had stopped. The hospital planned to send her home the next day. The baby was safe.

The next two weekends my emotions roller-coastered with hospital visits for miscarriage scares. The no contact judgment from the court was still in place, so David could never be there for support. Waiting for the results each time she sought medical help weighed on everyone, especially him.

On her next checkup, the message came. "The doctor says there is no heartbeat. The baby is gone. The doctor recommended a D&C, but I'm going home to miscarry naturally."

My heart sank. How was I going to tell David this news?

I asked Bob to bring David to my office where we took him downstairs away from the staff. The basement smelled musty as tears welled in my eyes. I looked into his youthful face and tried to find the words.

"What?" David's voice held frustration.

"I'm sorry, honey." I glanced at his dad who stood, hands in his pockets, watching solemnly. "The baby didn't make it."

A look of pain and devastation crossed David's face. He bolted up the flight of wooden steps and slammed the door as he exited the building. Bob and I looked at each other in dismay, not knowing how to console our son.

We followed David outside to see where he had gone. My storefront was located in the middle of the downtown strip mall with businesses on both sides. In the late afternoon sun, parked cars lined the street in front of the shops. But David was nowhere to be seen.

We walked up and down the sidewalk hoping to catch a glimpse of him. Then I saw movement in the front seat of my car. I sighed with relief and approached the car.

David sat in the passenger seat, arms locked across his knees, and face buried in his arms as he sobbed. I wrapped my arms around him. At first, he jerked away in anger, but I persisted, and he let me hold him.

"I am so, so sorry, honey." I held him tight with my cheek pressed against his soft hair.

Later that evening, I got an unexpected call from her. "I was playing with the dog on the floor and, all of a sudden, the baby kicked. The heartbeat must have just been too low for the doctor to hear."

My mind raced to take in what she was saying.

"If he would have done a D&C like he wanted," she continued, "the procedure would have killed the baby. They didn't even do bloodwork or an ultrasound."

On Monday, an ultrasound found the bottom chambers of the baby's heart were underdeveloped, but she was going to be all right.

"She could grow out of the heart problem," she said. "If not, a simple surgery will repair it."

She and David talked about suing the doctor. She had won a lawsuit for a large sum of money over the death of her little boy. Now, she had David convinced they needed to do the same with the misdiagnosis of the loss of the little girl.

I tried to explain mistakes happen, and doctors are not perfect but do their best. The doctor who told her there was no heartbeat was the same doctor who delivered David. I phoned the doctor's office and spoke with him. While he was currently not facing lawsuits, I was concerned this girl would initiate one.

The emotional ups and downs over the baby had become more than David could handle. He consumed more drugs and alcohol resulting in being put on house arrest again with another court date scheduled.

She sent pictures of cute baby girl clothing she purchased online. One evening, she excitedly shared plans for decorating the nursery including a white crib and the gold nameplate of Harper hung above the crib.

Pictures of 3D ultrasounds came, and I felt joy again.

"Look at this one. She has David's chiseled jaw," she pointed out. "She's going to look just like David."

I responded by sending pictures of David as a newborn, and we compared the resemblances. These were happy moments.

Then came Sunday night, February 10.

CHAPTER TWENTY-FOUR

Ice Storm

The weather consisted of ice and snow hitting our area. A storm moved in quickly, and school was canceled for the next day. Early in the evening, another text from his girlfriend's roommate pinged in.

"I'm worried. I came home and found her sitting on the bathroom floor crying. She's in a lot of pain. She's cramping really bad."

"Does she want to go to the hospital?" I texted back. "I can meet her there."

"Not yet."

"Have her try soaking in a hot bath," I suggested.

"If she goes to the hospital, she doesn't want to go to the local hospital. With the baby's heart condition, she plans to deliver in Indy."

She had been told because of the complications she was having, her medical team might have to take the baby early. For the baby to have a chance of survival, she just needed to get past twenty weeks.

The wind howled outside my window. "The weather is getting bad," I noted. "I suggest if she needs to go, we go now, or you won't be able to get to Indy."

"Her aunt is coming over to check on her."

I felt relieved because her aunt worked as a nurse at an OB/GYN office. "Good! Keep me posted."

Around 10:00 p.m., her roommate sent a photo of her sleeping. "I'm worried. I don't think she looks very good. What do you think?"

"Let me call and get an emergency release from detention for David," I replied. "They told us to call if there was an emergency for the baby. I'll bring David and meet at your place to take her to the hospital."

After a moment, the words appeared on the screen. "Not yet. I'll keep you informed."

I phoned David and told him to be prepared if I came to get him. I sat on the sofa and prayed for her and the baby and waited anxiously for the okay to go. But there was only silence for the rest of the night.

When I woke the next morning, I checked my messages. And there it was, a message I would never forget.

"I lost the baby. She's gone!"

I felt overcome with anger and grief at the same time. "Why didn't someone tell us so David could be there?"

"My mom was there, and I didn't want David to see me like that," she explained. "I held her, and we took photos."

"But David did not get to hold her. How is he supposed to get closure?" *How selfish could she be?* "Where is the baby now?"

"I'm sorry. I can't do this right now," she responded. "Please tell David for me."

Through anger and tears, I showered, applied makeup, and drove to town where David had stayed at a friend's house.

His best friend, Blaze, walked down the porch steps and leaned into my car's passenger window. "David's upstairs." He gave his characteristic smile.

"I need you to get him, please."

Blaze's smile disappeared, and he rushed back up the porch steps and disappeared into the house to get David. I dreaded this conversation. *How was he going to receive the news this time?* At least he was with friends today who could hopefully help him through.

Several minutes later, David came out of the house and got into the passenger side of the car.

"What?" There was an edge in his tone.

"She texted me this morning," I said softly. "She lost the baby last night."

Anger crossed his tired face. "She's probably just lying anyway." He jerked the handle to the car door and got out.

I was starting to feel the same way. What was the truth?

Despite what was or wasn't, that baby had been real to us, and we had both fallen in love with her before even meeting her. I internalized my grief. David drank more alcohol. We both needed closure.

That evening, I asked her to send photos of the baby. At first, she argued she was a private person and those were for her. I continued to explain David was the father and needed closure as well. He didn't get to hold her and say goodbye like she did. He at least needed to have some pictures.

She sent me four photos. One was little Harper, her skin tone red. She was lying on a warming blanket while she and her mom took turns holding her. The additional photos showed little fingers. So tiny. So lifeless.

I sat at the round oak kitchen table with a heavy heart and stared out the window at the yard fringed by the woods. I needed to find a way to help David if that was possible. On my phone, I did an internet search for the local coroner in her hometown and dialed the number.

"Sir, my son lost his child in a miscarriage the other night. The baby was only twenty weeks but is there any way we could get a death certificate? He's taking this really hard. I just want to try to help him find some closure."

"We don't typically give a death certificate at twenty weeks," he explained. "But Ma'am… I don't have a fetus here. I haven't had one in a few years."

"She miscarried at the hospital," I said. "Could you check please?"

"Let me make a phone call." He took my number. "I'll call you back."

"There was no miscarriage at that hospital that night," he reported when he called back. "Are you sure you have the right hospital?"

"I assumed she went to her hometown. Maybe she went to Indy." I thought of something else. "Can you tell me if there was a car accident last Friday night in your area?"

He consulted his information. "No, there is no record of one."

"She sent videos." I recalled, "Fire trucks and ambulances were there."

"This is crazy! In all my career, I have never heard of something like this. I'm sorry, I can't help you any further," he said apologetically. "I hope you can get answers for you and your son."

Disillusionment flooded my heart. Did she have the child and was hiding her? What did she do with the baby? Where was our Baby Harper?

Later, as I soaked in a bathtub, I gazed at the photos on my phone of this little one. When I first saw the ultrasound photos, I thought the baby was more developed for her age than expected. But I reasoned the new technology created better images.

I searched online and found the photos she sent had been pulled from the internet.

How does someone do this? Why would anyone jerk us through the emotional roller coaster she had us on for months? Had she sold the baby for money? What was she hiding?

An attorney told me there wasn't much he could do to help me find answers and shook his head in disbelief someone would go to such lengths to be deceptive.

I told him about the lawsuit she won over the death of her son and her desire to sue her current doctor.

He consulted computer files. "There is no record of any lawsuits filed or won under her name."

That evening, I drove to the police station in her hometown and asked to speak to an officer. "All I want to know is, where is the baby," I said. "Did she give birth and she's keeping it from us? Did she miscarry? If so, where is the baby? Is this whole insane thing a sick lie? I just want closure for our family."

The next day, the captain called. "I spoke with her. A woman has the right to have an abortion if she wants and the father has no rights. She has done nothing wrong."

Abortion? I couldn't grasp the concept. Weren't we *all* excited and planning for this child? Decorating, buying baby clothes, choosing a name? Was she lying to the officer now too?

David sunk deeper into drugs and alcohol. I realized how much I had been affected by this episode when I noticed a couple walking behind me on the sidewalk with their child. They held her hand and counted, "One, two, three, jump. One, two, three, jump." The little girl giggled as they swung her between them.

My heart sped up and my eyes flooded with tears. That could have been my grandchild. My son, swinging his little girl.

For weeks, the sight and sound of babies and little children caused a flood of emotions to bubble to the surface. I was left with a broken heart and no real answers.

Driving home, I told David, "I want to pursue putting her on the stand and get her to tell us the truth."

"Why, Mom?" David met my eyes. "Why destroy her life the way she's destroyed mine? Would that be right?"

My son had just shown me what true forgiveness looked like.

I was faced with a choice. Do *I* choose to forgive her? I knew it was what God would want, and if I didn't forgive, bitterness and anger would root in my own life and evil would win.

But I was so angry at her. So hurt. She didn't just hurt me, she hurt my son.

Sitting in the courtroom the following Monday made the choice to forgive more difficult. Now she wasn't the only one I needed to forgive. These people would make decisions regarding David's immediate future. Would he remain on house arrest or go to a new youth center?

Having learned about her lies, I shared the information with the court. Instead of the support I thought I would get, the probation officer once again used the new information to mock me in front of the judge and prosecutor.

"First, Mom tells us this girl is good for David," he bellowed across the courtroom. "Now, she's telling us this girl is crazy and wants her kept away from her son."

Feelings of defeat and embarrassment washed over me. Was there anyone we could turn to for help? It appeared the only goal these people had was to prove I was an unfit parent and send my son away. I wanted to trust them. Instead, I no longer trusted anyone with our truths.

CHAPTER TWENTY-FIVE

Break Through

Journal: Easter Sunday, April 21, 2019

This land you have given me, Lord, is so beautiful. I'm sitting on my porch looking over the pond and enjoying the beautiful sound of the red-wing blackbirds. Thank you for giving me this space for a season.

It's Easter Sunday. I had the pleasure of having Austin and his girlfriend go to church and a movie with me. I had the blessed opportunity to sit with my favorite aunt, Aunt Jane, at church.

Mom, Dad, Austin, Bob, and I visited David at the Youth Center. We played a family game. It felt good to laugh and see David smile. He took us on a tour of the facility and showed us his classrooms where he's doing online courses. I'm so proud of him; he's getting all A's.

When we left, I hugged him goodbye. He held me tight for a moment and told me thanks for coming. When I turned around, Mom and Dad were wiping away tears. When the bell rings and the cards and snacks are put away, the goodbyes are the hardest part of our visits.

After our visit with David, the three of us went to see *Break Through*. The movie was inspiring about a mom's fight to overcome her son's condition after he drowned. When I see such movies, I want to come out fighting to impact the lives of others to be overcomers through heartache, grief, loss, health issues, broken relationships, addictions, and disappointments.

I left the movie asking when is my turn because I have a story to share. When God, can I quit wasting time in a print shop and be used by you to make a difference. To do real ministry work. To use the talents you gave me to write, speak, and paint.

I know everything you have brought me through was for this calling. How long, Lord? How much more refining do I need?

I want to sit by the curb holding the lady after the accident. I want to listen to the angry woman whose husband left her. I want to pray with the lost and love the lonely.

I do thank you for giving me my dreams. It wasn't long ago I felt so grateful for everything. I had a beautiful home, I was provided for financially with little to worry about, I was given all the credit and finances needed to keep this home and buy my dream business.

I am not sure what I did wrong to mismanage it. Because it now feels like it's all being taken away.

I knew, Lord, when you let Mark slip away, through grief you showed me my purpose. I knew then I may have to lose everything. My soulmate, my boys to worldly things, my business, and my home. And I accepted that. I knew life was about to get tough. I just didn't know how tough.

Through these trials and horrible storms, I learned what I already knew but had never walked through or experienced. I own nothing, I control nothing, and I can count on no one but you. Anything here today can be gone tomorrow. The days I don't have enough strength to get off my knees, you lift and carry me through.

You are the only thing consistent. But even you can get quiet. It feels like you are not listening, but I know you are. I knew this would be hard, Lord, but I didn't realize how tired I would get and how badly it could affect me physically.

Lord, will you please allow me to do my calling soon? Write, paint, and speak. To be with my soulmate and travel and help people. I have no one to travel with and share my passion of you with. I will always rely on you, but will you please bless me now with the one appointed to be my companion? My helpmate, my soulmate. We have work to do, and I am anxious because I feel I am wasting my time, energy, and money on something that no longer matters. I don't want to do this alone. Who can I rejoice with at the end of the day?

Help me be patient while I wait on you. Help me not give up despite what others may say. Free me from anything holding me back, down, or in bondage. Thank you, Lord.

CHAPTER TWENTY-SIX

Sun rays and Rain

Journal: May 7, 2019

Lord, as I close out my old journal and start this new one, I am in a new season. One that has good new starts and scary things included.

Business is better. I have a new printer and a new sense of hope. Work is not as hard on me physically. I trust you will help us recover financially. For the sake of the employees, please don't let me fail. Bring the business to be greater than it has been.

Thank you for new customers, a great team to work with, and friends. Thank you for each week's provisions. Thank you for putting us back on top. Give us an incredible year where I can help others, where bonuses become common, and your kingdom is advanced.

Let me come up with products that sell and send a message to customers, my employees, and our community. The new *Cause-* is the Kingdom!

Journal: May 26, 2019

Saturday evening, I caught up the books so I could get taxes done. At 11:30 p.m. I compared January through May's sales to the sales from the previous year.

My heart sank to realize we may have to close the doors. We lost sixty thousand dollars in sales from last year. The leak had not stopped from the fallout of my ex-husband's illness. Our sales are still dropping. Why?

Two years ago, Lord, when I had the vision for the exposition of paintings, I felt Satan wasn't going to like this, and you said I may have to lose everything before it happens. My guy, my sons, my business, and my home. Well, that truly may be the case. I have lost the guy, I am losing the business, and then I will lose my home.

Lord, what am I to do?

I have lost everything. It's your voice I seek because I'm not sure what I feel *led* to do if you are still. I don't want to doubt. I don't want to question. But when I ask what to do and I get nothing in return, what do I do?

I can't keep ignoring this business problem. I can't keep holding on to dreams when I see nothing that appears to be you. I know we are to have faith, trust, and wait. But how do I hold on when everything is falling apart and the only one I have to lean on and count on won't speak or show me the next step to take?

What do I do about this business? I am tired, struggling, out of money, and have bills. I do not want to be unwise, lazy, or irresponsible. I want to take whatever steps you want me to. I just can't hear or feel your leading. Why are you leaving me alone? I understand you are working ahead of me and watching to see if I trust you and will remain in faith.

I will always trust you and always have faith in you, your provision, and your love. My question is how do I step if you do not lead or confirm I'm heading in the right direction?

I am alone in all of this and only have you, so please speak to me. Please give me a new fresh revelation.

I wanted God to speak in a way I knew it was for sure, Him. I continued to hear preachers talk about reading the Word and hearing from God. I didn't know how God would answer my question this time, but I needed something from Him.

Not sure where to begin, I flipped open to where I had a bookmark in my *Mom's Devotional Bible.*

On the left page was a devotion, *Praying and Waiting.* "There are so many ways in which God's actions or inactions make little sense to us. We ask for help, and he is silent. We trust in him to provide, and he withholds. But is God inconsistent, or is he simply running according to another time schedule, another set of priorities?"

Noting Habakkuk questioned God's plan, the devotional said, "We must pray with a willingness to wait and wait with a willingness to pray."

Habakkuk 2:1-3 says, "I will stand at my watch and station myself on the ramparts; I will look to see what he will say to me, and what answer I am to give to this complaint. Then the Lord replied: Write down the revelation and make it plain on tablets so that a herald may run with it. For the revelation awaits an appointed time; it speaks of the end and will not prove false. Though it linger, wait for it; it will certainly come and will not delay."

As I read, I found hope. I read and reread this passage while waiting in the stillness of God. I had this scripture now, and I prayed for strength and clarity. Most of all, I prayed for a fresh revelation to write down and hold.

From the sofa, I peered out the window over the land I dearly loved. So much had happened since that night I said yes to His call.

I prayed, "Lord, if I lose the business, I can't afford this house. But I love this house. This became our safe place where no one could kick out me or my boys. I designed it, chose the colors and the lights and the cabinets. It was my dream home. We've made good memories here for my boys with friends four-wheeling, fishing, and sleepovers in the basement. I'm not ready to give it up. Please don't make me leave until you've prepared my heart. I know you said I may have to be willing to give it up, and it looks like that is going to happen, but not yet please. I'll put the house up for sale when it's time, but let me stay a while longer. Help prepare my heart for that day, and I'll be okay."

Journal: July 4, 2019

God is moving rapidly and things are selling rapidly. Both embroidery machines and the truck brought enough money to pay off the two small loans. That is refreshing. I have reached a peace about selling my home, and it's up for sale. I'm ready to see where God is taking me.

Journal: October 2019

God has done so much for me in recent months.

With three weeks left before I have to move, I have no home to move to. I visited nice apartment complexes, called on decent rental property, and keep running into roadblocks. All I can do is trust God's timing to provide.

I put a post on social media asking if anyone knew of anything. For income reasons, I couldn't buy until the first of the year and taxes would be done. Renting was my only option. A customer said he had a property in Marion. I didn't want Marion, but it was a nice home in a nice neighborhood for slightly more than the amount I had budgeted.

I felt hopeful but nervous about the high payment.

Recalling my friend lived in the same neighborhood as the potential renter, I texted to ask my friend questions about the housing addition. He offered me his place to rent for the amount I had budgeted along with a link to photos.

I recalled surveying my home and saying, "Lord, do I have to lose all of this? I picked these cabinets, the countertops, these lights. Where will I go that I can have these things I enjoy? Where will I get another home with this big of a bedroom?"

When I walked into my friend's house, I knew God had handpicked this one for me. The cabinets were the same color, with counters and lights like I had. The bedroom was larger than the one I owned. God gave me extras including a vaulted ceiling, fireplace, a loft for a painting studio, storage space in the attic, and a garden tub I sacrificed when I built my home to allow for the ex's desires.

The only thing missing was the privacy of being on land, but the neighborhood was quiet with friendly people.

Additionally, the Lord provided the necessary help to move and additional money from the sale of items to allow me to buy nice new things for the new place. It felt wonderful to have the funds to buy what I wanted.

I felt blessed to have family and friends help me move. Amazingly, the people who bought my house offered to help in any way they could. They burned trash, kept items I couldn't move, and helped on moving day.

I prayed for the house to sell to those God had chosen to own the property after me. When I met them, there was absolutely certainty I could walk away from that address knowing it was their turn to enjoy the gift of that home.

They shared they wanted the house before they set foot on the property. After touring the house and property, they pulled out of the drive yelling out the window, "It's sold!"

One evening, I went to the house to pick up some of my residual things.

"Valerie, I want you to know our church is praying for you and your boys." The new owners said, "Smile. It'll be okay."

God gave double in return for my loss through people and possessions. I was blessed through trial and now testimony. He provided a better home, perfect timing, the finances to move, and more.

CHAPTER TWENTY-SEVEN

Lightning Strikes

Journal: October 20, 2019

Only two months ago, I was in Dallas visiting Mark. Since then, I sold my house, the boys were arrested, Mark and I stopped talking for a while, and I moved into a temporary house owned by an old friend from church.

Both boys were picked up and sent away. Losing both at the same time is more than any mom's heart should have to deal with, especially during a season of holidays to come.

David

I was about to turn seventeen when I went to boys school. In my senior year of high school, I was doing what I normally did on the weekend—get high and drink with my homies.

I invited two guys to my house, and we listened to music, then decided to leave the house just to go do something. It was evening and dark outside in our quiet little subdivision.

I don't remember our intentions, but while walking, we decided to car hop which means getting into parked cars and stealing whatever objects we found.

I was always sketched out thinking somebody would just happen to walk outside while I was in their car. But I did it anyway. Not even five minutes into our walk, we found something.

We were still in my housing addition, which I didn't like because the cops always came to my house because I used to ding dong ditch a lot where I'd ring a neighbor's doorbell and run away before they could answer the door. But we just happened to hit a couple of cars on the way out of the area. And there it was—a gun.

We didn't even think to search the rest of the car. We grabbed the gun and ran. It was just a little black .22, but now I walked around like I was the man. Having found the gun, we looked in every car in sight hoping to find something valuable.

At nearly 6:00 in the morning, we went back to my house. After hours of searching cars, we found a few dollar bills. But with the gun, we felt it was a successful night. Exhausted after our long night, we dropped into bed to get some sleep.

Austin

The bright red and blue lights lit my back window. The squad car that had followed as I drove through town signaled me to pull over. I veered to the right, came to a slow stop alongside the curb, and put the gear shift in park.

Through my rearview mirror, I watched the uniformed officer step out of his vehicle with a flash light in hand and approach my Malibu. I rolled down the window and waited to hear why I was being stopped. I hadn't done anything wrong this time.

"Step out of the car, please."

I unfastened my seat belt, opened my car door, and slowly stepped out to stand next to my car.

"I need to see your driver's license."

I pulled my wallet from my back pocket and handed my license to the officer.

He glanced past me into my car. "Where are you headed?"

"To a friend's house," I replied.

"Someone called in suspicious activity down the street." He eyed me. "What do you know about it?"

I shrugged. "I don't know what you're talking about."

"Were you involved in breaking into cars?" He added, "Stealing a gun?"

"No!" I shook my head

"Do you have any guns?"

"No."

The officer pressed. "You're sure you weren't involved?"

I insisted I didn't know what he was talking about.

"You can go," he dismissed. "But stay out of trouble, Austin."

I climbed back in the car to see if I could find David and his friends. But I didn't find them, so I went to visit one of my friends at his house.

All I knew about what the officer asked was this time the problem wasn't me.

David

After we woke up the next morning, we called one of our homies to take us to the nearby big city where we met friends at the shopping mall.

We walked around peering into the stores for a while, rode the escalator to grab something to eat in the food court, and decided to find a place to shoot the gun.

The five of us piled into one vehicle and drove out to the corn and bean fields that cover the countryside in our part of state. One by one, we rolled down our windows and took turns shooting the .22 into the air. I felt exhilarated.

After shooting, we took the two guys we met at the mall back to their car in the mall parking lot. My homies needed to go home, so I called Austin and told him and his friend to meet me at the park where I would be dropped off.

We arrived at the park at about the same time. I climbed into the passenger seat of Austin's car and pulled the gun from my backpack. "Look what I got."

"Holy s$%t!" Austin's eyes grew big. "Where'd you get that?"

"I went car hopping last night with friends." I explained with a grin. "Drive me out to the country and I'll let you get some fun in shooting it."

Austin drove to the country, and we took turns shooting into the woods. Back inside city limits, our friend rolled down his window, pointed the gun toward a house, and pulled the trigger.

Bang!

"What the f@#k are you doing!" Austin yelled at him.

"You shot at a person's house." I looked to see if anyone had noticed. "In the middle of town."

That night, I wanted to go car hopping to see if we could find something else. Austin didn't want to go after he had been questioned about this exact activity last night.

"Go with us, Austin," I said. "We need you to drive."

"No! I got pulled over last night because of you guys," he stated. "They thought it was me."

"Come on," I begged. "The guys are already here."

With a sigh, he gave in.

Once it was dark, we went uptown to a richer area of town where we hadn't looked the night before. Austin parked on a side street, and we got to work. Austin walked with us but didn't get into the cars. He was just there to be the driver.

At first, we found mostly pocket change and phone chargers. Then we found cans of beer. We didn't want to carry it around, so we threw the beer in Austin's car and went to the next parked car.

When we found a cooler full of liquor, we decided to go home and drink.

"Austin, take the cooler back to the car and wait for us there," I outlined. "We'll hit the cars that are on our way back."

My friend was on one side of the street, and I was on the other. I was getting into a car when a guy came out of his house across the street. I went about my business acting like it was my car.

"Hey, what are you doing?" he yelled from across the street. "Get out of there!"

I nonchalantly walked away, forgetting about my buddy who was in the dude's truck parked beside his house.

I caught up to Austin who was still carrying the cooler. "Run!"

Austin dropped the cooler, and we sprinted toward the car and sped away. We skirted into the alley to see if our friend got away. Thinking about the cooler, I thought we needed to grab it because it held our fingerprints. I hopped out of the car, ran through someone's yard, and scrunched down behind trees to see if I could grab the cooler. But the cooler wasn't there.

I sprinted back to the car, and we circled the block to find our friend. I couldn't call because he left his cell phone at my house. As Austin drove home, I hoped my friend found his way back.

On the way, a cop pulled behind us. We had the pocket change, pot, and trinkets we found in cars lying on the seat between us. The pack of beer sat under my feet in the front passenger seat.

"Austin, just drive good, and we'll be fine." Inside I was freaking out.

Austin remained quiet, focused on driving well and not drawing attention. If we were pulled over, we would be caught with possession of stolen goods, pot, and alcohol. We both had already had possession charges and had spent time locked away.

The cop car followed us to the road where we lived, but when we turned down our street, the cop continued straight. We breathed a sigh of relief, took everything inside the house, and unloaded it in my bedroom.

We turned on a movie while hoping our friend didn't get caught. We each cracked open a beer and lit a blunt to smoke the pot we found.

An hour later, I heard a knock at my bedroom window. I went to the window with the blind pulled halfway up but couldn't see anyone. I lifted the bottom pane of the window to find a gun pointed at my face.

CHAPTER TWENTY-EIGHT

Sunk

"What the h@!! Bro!" It was our friend. "Point that somewhere else. Where'd you get that?"

"In the truck where that guy came out." He started to tell us. "I was in his truck beside his house when he yelled at you. I saw he was distracted with you, so I hurried and searched the glove box and found the gun in there. Then I took off."

He walked all the way back to our house and observed, "The cops are all over."

The gun was a .45 and shiny. Now we had two.

Sunday, we met up with some of our people to roadie (cruise) and shoot the guns. With ammunition we found in the vehicles, we drove to the country, shooting out the car windows across the fields and into the blue sky.

We pulled over by a cornfield so I could pee. A truck pulled up beside us.

The driver called, "Are you guys shooting guns?"

One of my friends thought quickly. "No, it was just firecrackers."

The guy drove to the end of the road, turned around, and drove back the way he had come.

"Bro...come on!" I said to my friend who came up with the lame story. "Firecrackers? Like the guy was going to believe that."

That night, we went car hopping again but didn't find anything valuable. I had to get back to the house early because I had school the next morning. We drove everyone home, and Austin dropped me off. I got left with the guns.

Austin

I had just gotten off probation and decided tonight I'd join my friends and smoke pot. I had been hitting some dabs when my cell phone rang.

"Austin Rigdon?" asked the voice on the other end.

"Yeah?"

The caller identified himself a police officer. "We need you to come down to the annex."

I had no idea why I was being called to the police annex.

"Okay." I hung up, and the next thing I knew, I was waking up on the floor of the barn. I had passed out, landed on my back, and took a hard hit to my head against the concrete floor. Once I regained consciousness, my friend took my hand and pulled me to a standing position. I was confused as to what just happened. I had no idea why I passed out except maybe something in the dabs I smoked caused it.

I walked outside into the nighttime air and left the barn and my friends behind. I got into the car and pulled onto the country road to drive downtown to the police annex building where they do interrogations.

On the drive, I felt anxious, not knowing what the police wanted to question me about this time. I hoped they wouldn't notice I was high. Of all the times, it had to be the first time I smoked weed after I got off probation.

Turning onto the street to the annex, their parking lot was in sight when flashing lights turned on behind me. A cop car was attempting to pull me over.

I parked, and an officer got out of the cruiser and approached the driver's side of the vehicle. I rolled down my window.

The officer looked past me and into my car. "Did you know your headlights are off?"

"No." I didn't believe my headlights were off.

"I need you to step out of the vehicle."

The officer searched my car and found a bullet. It must have fallen out of the box when we drove to the country to shoot in the woods.

The officer escorted me inside the annex building and into a small room. I was interrogated for four grueling hours.

David

After Austin dropped me at home, I went straight to my bedroom. I put the two guns in my backpack next to my bed. Tomorrow, I would find a place to hide them.

I woke at 2:00 a.m. to find cops standing over me.

"Where is it?" the officer demanded.

Coming out of a deep sleep, I replied, "Where is what?"

"Where is the gun?"

"I don't know what you are talking about."

They took me out of the room while they searched every drawer, closet shelf, under my bed, and lifted my mattress. Finally, an officer unzipped my backpack.

"Why are guns in your school bag?" The officer's questions implied I had plans to shoot something at school.

"I put them in my backpack until morning," I said. "I didn't have time to hide them before I went to bed."

They told me to get dressed, placed handcuffs on my wrists, and escorted me to the police car parked along the curbside. At the police annex building, I was led to the too familiar interrogation room.

The officer sat across from me and fired questions. "Where did you get the guns?"

Scared, I hesitated.

He repeated, "Where did you get them?"

"I went out car hopping," I said. "I found them in the cars."

"Who were you with?"

"You already know." I nodded to a yellow sticky note in front of him listing our names.

"What were you doing with the guns?"

"I took them out in the country and shot them."

"What were you planning to do with them?"

"I don't know," I considered. "Sell them or something."

The conversation went on forever as he asked the same questions and I gave him the same answers. Then he left.

I waited. Finally, I was put in the back of the cop car and transferred to the Detention Center.

Austin and David were charged with possession and theft of a firearm. Their friends who took part were questioned, but, as far as we know, not charged; including the one who shot at the house.

The first time I drove to the Detention Center to visit David, the place didn't look much different than the other buildings we had been to.

Accompanied by my mom and Bob, I entered the lobby where a lady at a small desk asked us to sign in. We were instructed to place our possessions in a locker. Along with other visitors, we took seats in two rows facing each other in a line for the metal detectors. I felt awkward sitting across from complete strangers. The room was quiet until a few ladies struck up a conversation and others chimed in.

At 7:00 p.m., we lined up to walk through metal detectors and pass by the stern guard holding his wand.

Walking down the long corridor felt like a school hallway, but everything changed once I passed through the big steel door.

Inside, the two-story hall were cell doors with small windows. I could see inmates behind the glass. The thought of my David sitting in one of these cells caused emotions to rise, and I wanted to cry. But now wasn't the time for crying. I was about to see my son.

In an old gymnasium, chairs were placed twelve feet apart. Facing each seat was a group of chairs for visitors to sit across from their inmate. Instructions included do not look at other inmates. I was not allowed to hug or touch my son as I had been allowed to do at the residential facilities.

I pushed back tears when I saw him waiting for us in his gray sweatsuit. His head had been shaved nearly bald.

A smile crossed his face when he saw us. How I wanted to hug his neck!

We tried to find things to talk about. As we gave David updates from the outside world, I felt uncomfortable sitting in our little pod in the middle of this big and noisy gymnasium.

Suddenly, a young man yelled something I couldn't make out at what appeared to be his parents. He threw back his chair, but the guards immediately stepped in and escorted him out. Reading the embarrassment on their faces as they left the area, I felt bad for his parents.

When our visit ended, we gathered our belongings from the small lockers and waited to be let out of the locked building. We were the last ones to exit into the cool night air where family members were getting into their cars and driving away.

A flood of emotions hit so hard I couldn't take another step. I stopped in the middle of the sidewalk, dropped with my hands on my knees, and burst into tears. Mom and Bob waited in silence while I tried to catch my breath.

With each new placement, the facility got worse. *What would the next one be like?*

Journal: October 20, 2019

Austin is out on bail and working. We are sure he'll be serving time in jail after he returns to court in November.

David is in the YOC Detention Center and goes to court in a little over a week to find out his location of placement and length of time to serve. He will be gone until he's at least eighteen. The state is pushing for the Department of Corrections, Pendleton Juvenile Center, which is a state youth prison. I am praying for White's Juvenile Center, a youth residential. There he will be able to go to school and graduate with a diploma and not just a GED. At White's, he will attend church, and my prayer is the Lord can reach him there.

Though this is difficult to feel so out of control regarding the lives of my children, I know God has a plan and will use all this for good. It's now my storm, but also my testimony. I can't control any of this and have to fully trust God will intervene where, when, and how it is needed. I continue to guide, love, and pray over them.

Mark decided to be friends and stay single. He isn't sure if it's the right decision or one he'll regret, but he says if he doesn't test remaining as a single man first, he'll always look back and wonder if it was the better way for him. Though it hurts and I feel rejected again, I believe he is right. I'd rather he lived through this stage, so it doesn't cause us problems in the future if we were to reunite and marry.

My challenge now is do I continue to believe the promises?
Should I not date and wait on him? Or accept he made a choice,
I wasn't it, and after seven years of waiting, I need to move on.

CHAPTER TWENTY-NINE

The Hurricane Erupts

In the middle of the night, the sound of the turning doorknob interrupted my sleep.

I heard the door creak open. *David is walking in. I wonder what he wants. No, it feels like Austin.*

He came to the bedside and stood over me.

Why is he just standing there? Why isn't he saying anything? I'm so tired. I just want to sleep.

Then I felt something different surround me, and I realized the presence was not Austin. An evil presence sat beside me. I felt warm breath on my bare arm and froze in fear. Too afraid to move, I held my breath as the terror set in.

I saw myself float out of my body and look down from the ceiling. I could see myself lying in bed.

Then I saw a demon hunched on his knees beside me. He laughed. Then he ran his tongue slowly up my arm. He pressed his index finger into my forearm and firmly held it there.

"Hahahahaha." His laugh was sinister. "I'm not done with your boys. And I'm not done with you either."

"God," I screamed. "Help!"

Immediately, I was back in my body and awake. I flipped over to see who was next to me. No one was there, but I could feel his finger pressed into my arm. I tried to calm my breathing and relax, but sleep did not come easy.

The next morning, the demon's warning caused such deep emotional distress all I could do was cry. I called the office and told them I wouldn't be in.

"God, David goes to court tomorrow, and I'm so scared this is going to go bad." I grabbed a box of tissues and sat on the living room sofa in my pajamas. "Lord, David can't go to the DOC. He's not a bad enough kid to be put in a facility like that. Please have the judge send him to White's where he can graduate with a diploma. They'll make him attend church and maybe, God, you could reach him there. Please, God! I'm so scared."

I cried. "Satan told me he's still after my boys. If David goes to Pendleton, what bad will come out of there? Will he die in there? There's school shooters and hard drug dealers in that place. Please, God, I am begging you! Help us tomorrow. Touch the heart of this judge. Protect David. I know I'm not supposed to live in fear, and I know I need to trust you, but this fear I feel is paralyzing. Your will be done and not mine. Please help us!"

For the next twenty-four hours, I felt the demon's finger pressing into my arm as a constant reminder.

The following day, Bob and I waited in the courthouse corridor for our turn. The elevator opened and out stepped an officer. Several inmates shuffled behind him, chains on their wrists and around their ankles. Last to appear was David.

He glanced our way and flashed a smile. I prayed he'd still be smiling at the end of this day. We had a fill-in attorney who briefly came over to discuss his plan of action. He would request White's Institute for David. Prison was too extreme for what he needed, and our goal was to allow him to finish school and graduate, surpassing the GED he'd receive at the Department of Corrections.

The courtroom door opened, and an officer called David's name. It was our turn to go before the judge.

We took seats at a long wooden table to the left of the bench. The prosecutor and probation officer were across from us on the right side of the room, and in the box were viewers, recording clerks, and detention officers.

Our attorney requested the facility where we wanted David sent, arguing at Whites he could finish high school and earn a diploma, setting him up for a better future. Whites was closer to home, making it easier for the family to support him, which was previously a goal of the courts and ours.

"David had plenty of opportunities to get his education prior to this. It's too late for that now," the prosecutor said. "He's a danger to the community, and the state requests he be sent to the Department of Corrections."

The prosecutor and probation officer brought up news of the emotionally messed up girlfriend and twisted everything we did as parents into the ultimate picture of bad parenting. The words of affirmation Bob and I received as parents from every facility we had been to, took an ugly turn that day.

The court opened the opportunity to take the stand and speak a word to the judge in David's defense. I had already determined I would fight for him no matter what. The kid might have made bad choices, but now we were talking about his future, and which facility would play a role in shaping how that future looked.

As they called me to the stand, my nerves were already a wreck feeling the weight of being attacked as a mother. My knees grew weak as I walked to the podium with the prosecutor and probation officer sitting directly behind. All eyes were on me from every corner of the room.

When I began to speak, a boldness and courage came out even *I* didn't know where it came from. I fought against the prosecutor and probation officers' arguments David was dangerous and needed to be in prison.

"I am begging you not to send David to the DOC." I broke into tears but was determined to fight my way through. "Yes, David has gotten into trouble with drugs and alcohol. But you haven't seen the David I know. David is full of compassion. Yes, he got mean with me when he was lit up and high on something, but that's not normally David. This is the kid who used his allowance to buy his friends pizza because their families couldn't afford it. This is the kid who used to use his allowance to take his friends to the skating rink or the movies because they'd never get to go otherwise. David has a good heart, you just haven't seen that side of him yet. He's smart and he deserves to graduate with a diploma. He just got caught in drugs and needs some help. I am begging you, please do not send him to the DOC. He's not that bad of a kid. He doesn't deserve prison."

I started to step away from the podium to return to my seat. The judge reached forward, I thought to hand me something, so I stopped and looked toward him. He wasn't reaching for me but for a tissue. He wiped tears streaming down his face.

I returned to my seat and grabbed my own tissue from the box sitting on our table. The room was quiet as the judge gathered his thoughts and shuffled through his papers.

I had the closing statement. I actually brought the judge to tears. Surely, I have won the argument.

"David, I sentence you to one year in the Juvenile Department of Corrections Center. You cannot continue to go down this path," the judge declared. "Your mother sees something good in you. I hope after your time is served, you can come back and be a good servant in this community." The judge banged the gavel.

No! This can't be happening. David got caught up in the drugs and needs some help. This is going to make it worse.

Shocked, I couldn't believe my ears.

The officer who stood at the side of the room witnessing the whole thing was a long-time friend of the family. He had worked with my dad for the sheriff's department, and I spent many evenings at his home as a young girl. My mom and his wife were best friends. His head dropped, and then he walked onto the platform with the shackles in his hands.

Most of the courtroom had cleared. Bob, David, and I were left alone with the attorney and the officer. The old family friend motioned for David, and he put the cuffs across his wrists. David kneeled on a chair and the officer cuffed his ankles. The sound of the clanging chains and the sight of my son being shackled was too much.

I quickly turned away, tightly squeezing my eyes closed. Everything suddenly went silent and the room began to spin. *Oh, God, help! I can't breathe. Don't let me pass out in front of everyone.*

I could no longer hear anything except the ringing in my ears. Tears ran down my face, as I held my hand over my mouth, trying to keep a sob from breaking loose. Someone gently touched my arm. I opened my eyes to see Bob.

With compassion in his eyes, the attorney said, "I know this is hard. I've seen these things before, and it's really for the best. It's going to be okay."

I saw motion on the ground floor. They already had walked David off the platform, and he dragged the chains with his shuffling feet while leaving the room. I had missed that hug goodbye! I had missed saying goodbye to my Davie.

I stepped into the hall and ran into our appointed attorney. She had heard the verdict.

"I have a really bad feeling about this," I told her.

"So do I," she replied.

Sitting on my couch that evening, surrounded by used tissues, I prayed. "Lord, what will come of David in there? I have such a bad feeling about this. Maybe it's the dream with the demon causing this fear or maybe it's you preparing my heart for the worst. Please help me with this anxiousness I feel. Will he be hurt in there? Will he come out alive? Will he come home worse than he was as he meets new drug dealers, hardcore criminals, and murderers? Will he survive? Why didn't they put him in a program that would give us hope and help him? Not prison!"

The disappointment and fear were raw when it was time for the first visit to the DOC. Bob drove the hour to the large brick buildings. As we turned into the facility, my heart shattered. Fences circled the campus consisting of one-story brick buildings. A watchtower rose in the middle of the grounds. Circles of barbed wire lined the fence walls. My boy was officially a prisoner.

Oh, God! I can't do this. My son needed rehab. Not this.

There was a miscommunication about the paperwork, and they would not let us visit David on that trip. Though disappointed, I was also relieved. As we drove away, there was no stopping my tears that flowed all the way home. I was nowhere near ready to see David in that place or to let him see me in that condition. By the next visit, my heart would be more prepared. I'd be able to handle the sights better. Better for David.

Once again, we signed in at the front counter. This time, a wall of glass separated visitors from the guards sitting at their computer monitors. I made sure I brought enough quarters to empty our pockets and house our IDs during the visit, and the rest would buy snacks from the vending machines.

We were led into another long room with a conveyor belt that felt like airport security. I removed my shoes and quarters and placed them in the white tubs and onto the belt that rolled through the security camera. At the other end, I sat on the single bench to put on my shoes after passing through the metal detector.

At the next locked door, I was ushered into a small middle holding room where visitors waited for the door to the commons to be unlocked.

Inside, the boys sat in chairs spread out in pods. David faced forward toward the attending guard while his dad and I faced him with a small wooden box for a table between us.

We let him get snacks from the vending machines that lined two of the walls. Then he taught us new card games. The hour felt short, but I looked forward each week to playing games, hearing about his school progress, and learning about the latest fight outbreak.

At the first visit, I watched a quiet and shy young man meet with a man I assumed was his father. I felt sorry for his dad because I knew the story. The boy's name was spread across the news. He was the most recent school shooter.

I felt concerned for David. I also felt concerned about threats on our lives from the inmates trying to pick fights with David.

CHAPTER THIRTY

Be Light

Life became calm and quiet with both boys incarcerated. Too quiet.

The Christmas season felt incredibly tough emotionally. My mom came for a visit in November. She normally came around Thanksgiving, and we would put up the tree with the kids and fill the house with beautiful decorations.

But decorating didn't feel right this year.

One evening, Mom asked, "Aren't you going to put up the tree?"

"No."

"Why not?"

"I don't feel like it." I fished for words. "The boys won't be home this year."

I worked the next day and came home to find Mom had gone into the attic and pulled out my Christmas village. The lighted houses were beautifully arranged on the floor in front of my fireplace and surrounded by a layer of decorative snow. I was quite surprised, but there was something more.

"Thanks, Mom," I told her. "I don't remember having that many houses."

"I brought mine because I thought maybe they would make you feel better." She added, "I want you to keep them."

My heart melted with her display of compassion and motherly love.

Those would be the only Christmas decorations that year in my house.

Mom and I liked to watch movies together, particularly true stories. She had watched one earlier that day and insisted we watch it together.

Faith by Potatoes was about a Scottish man living in Africa. Called to preach, he didn't wait twenty years to have someone invite him to preach. He sought out the opportunity by going to churches and asking to speak. God was faithful to bring the people and opportunity.

Second, he asked for the football stadium, rounded up the local farmers, and brought them together to pray for rain and crops. Did God want me to round up people in my town to pray for our children and these drug and alcohol curses?

Later that week, I turned off the lights in the little village houses. After I soaked in a hot tub, praying and pondering about speaking, I passed by and noticed the house on the end of the miniature village was back on. I turned it off again and went to bed.

The next morning, all the little houses were lit except the one that came on the night before. These houses were all on the same power strip while the house on the end was plugged into the outlet.

How could this be and why?

The houses had been set up for two weeks, and the lights had easily turned off and on as expected. Until now. I played with the power strip button, but it wasn't loose. I asked several friends about electricity, and they had no explanation.

Puzzled, I sat on the corner of the coffee table and stared at the lights. Was this another sign? A sign for what? I recalled the night when my Jesus painting was turned face down twice as I was warned about Austin getting into trouble.

Why would that spirit be in this house right now?

Texting with Mark, I described what happened.

"Why does everyone think of evil when something strange occurs? Our guardian angels send messages, too." He texted, "What were you thinking about when it happened?"

"You and I were texting about whether it was time for me to speak or wait."

Looking at the houses bright with warmth and invitation, I heard, "Bring light and hope to others."

I remembered the dates Mom and I noticed on the bottom of the little houses. I bought her first house as a Christmas gift exactly twenty years before. Twenty years ago I heard the holy spirit tell me at a Beth Moore conference, "You're going to be on that stage one day." That year, I knew I was being called to be a Christian speaker.

The little houses remained in place for the next four weeks. The lights never again came on by themselves.

The last line in the movie was, "Faith like potatoes. You can feel it. You can smell it. It is real. We need to have faith like potatoes. Your faith in God must be like it."

CHAPTER THIRTY-ONE

The Voyage

A year after I attended the Wycliffe Associates banquet, I researched the organization and trained to teach others how to use Wycliffe's methods and resource tools.

We made plans for me to join John on his team's next trip out of the States. Papers, shots, passports, insurance, fundraisers, and training—preparing to volunteer was a lengthy process. With each step, I grew more excited to see what God had in store.

A December trip came into focus, but the funds didn't line up. I called John and expressed my disappointment and frustration.

"Sometimes when these things happen, it's just not the right time," John reassured. "It doesn't mean it isn't going to happen. God's timing is always perfect."

The next morning, I turned on my TV to listen to televangelist Joyce Meyer, as I readied for work. On my screen was a satellite view of half of the earth blacked out except one continent. Brightly lit in gold color was Africa.

My heart felt the Holy Spirit say, "Don't worry. You're going to Africa."

John's team was scheduled to go to Congo, Africa. I was invited to join, and this time the needed funds came in. Prayers were spoken over the trip in our Sunday school class, and the support from dear friends encouraged me.

As I walked out of class and into the church gymnasium, I offered my arm to help my elderly friend, Bucky, walk to the sanctuary.

"Valerie. I'm so proud of you." A prayer warrior who never married, Bucky made me feel special. "I love you."

"I love you, too, Bucky," I said as she took my arm. "How do we do this?"

"Do what?"

"How do we travel halfway around the world, me a single woman and him a married man?" There appeared to be concern from leaders in the church.

"Oh, don't you go there!" Her voice echoed through the gymnasium. "I saw how your face lit up when you told me God called you to this. If John's wife had a problem with you going, you wouldn't be. It's the safest way for you to go. I have been a single woman all my life. There were times I had to rely on men to help me accomplish what God called me to do. If other people have a problem with it, that's their problem. You be obedient. You go."

With her words, my worry lifted.

I met with John's family many times during the year, and they became like family to me. The Sunday before we were to leave, John and I discussed arrangements for how and where to meet at the airport.

"You two are making this too hard," his wife interrupted. "We'll pick you up in the morning."

February 12, 2020. Day 1: Flight to Africa

Our day started at 5:30 a.m.

At the airline, the kiosk required the credit card used to purchase the ticket. I explained to the clerk I didn't bring that card with me.

"You have to have it to validate the ticket," the clerk explained.

He called his supervisor who tried an override. "I don't know that there is anything we can do."

Last week, there had been two unexplained charges, so the card was canceled. The bank expedited the process, so I had the card to buy my airline ticket. That required setting up a new account. Somehow my card number was saved as my login.

This morning, when I couldn't get the online login for my new credit card to work, I decided to wait until I returned from the trip to straighten out the account. I was able to show the clerk my phone contained the card number validating it was my card.

The supervisor went to see what could be done. I began to panic and texted people to pray. *What if I can't get on this flight? All this planning and now I can't go over a dumb card.*

I stopped and asked myself, *What are you doing? If God wants you to go, he'll take care of it. He got you this far.*

I calmly watched to see what God would do.

The supervisor came out of the office and nodded to a clerk. The next thing I knew the young man tagged my bags and let me go on.

February 14th, 2020. Day 2: Valentine's in the Congo

Today was physically tough. My body is not coping well with the time change.

Our facilitators are important chaplains of the Congo. Police, Army, Air Force, the Director of Chaplains, and I met the director of the Evangelical Church of Congo who invited us here. I feel small, but they greeted me with respect and kindness.

Lord, I am not sure why I am here. What good am I to these people? I do not speak their language. I do not know the system, and I don't even remember the software.

I feel so inadequate. What is my purpose? What is it you want me to see? To learn? To do? I can't even remember their names.

February 15, 2020. Day 3: Prayer

Today, I was sent back to the group with the director of our team.

Toward the end of our session, the facilitators, who all spoke French, got confused about how to divide the chapters in their Scriptures. With the language barrier, I wasn't sure what the problem was, so I asked a teammate to explain what the confusion was about.

Once I understood the problem, I asked the translator to speak for the director who could only speak English. With that suggestion, they got the problem worked out. That was the first time I felt useful.

We were wrapping up for the day when I heard the Director of Chaplains thanking the director, and then I heard him mention my name. A translator on my team spoke to me.

"They want you to pray over them," he translated for me.

"Me?"

"Yes," he nodded. "I will translate."

Me? The white woman pray over high-ranking military officials?

They prayed aloud their own prayers and my heart raced. Then, I prayed and my nerves calmed and my words were clear.

"Lord Jesus, I ask you to give each of these men wisdom and discernment. Give them strength as leaders with those they oversee to accomplish this task. Protect them and their families, for we know the enemy will be against this work. Thank you for this opportunity to serve you in the great commission. We love you. Now please, use us to share your love with others. In Jesus name, Amen."

After supper, I sat by the hotel pool. It was a beautiful night with a cool breeze, and music played in the background. I spent the evening pondering and writing in my journal.

I didn't realize what was taking place while my leg was crossed and my ankle was exposed to the night air.

February 17, 2020. Day 4: In the Congo

Today we were taken to the school compound where we trained the army to use the methods and resources to translate two languages into the language of the Congo military.

Driven by the army in a military jeep, I watched as they wove in and out of traffic, making everyone stop for them. I felt like a celebrity in a motorcade.

When we stepped out of the jeep at the school, I heard the children and their teachers in another wing of the compound. Before this trip is over, I want to meet the teachers and children.

They held a ceremony in our honor to kick off the workshops and introduced us individually. I felt out of place in the presence of generals, corporals, and majors. The President of the Evangelical Church of the Congo was surrounded by bodyguards. He was the one who asked Wycliffe to come and train his soldiers in the process of translating the Scriptures. I was humbled when he greeted me after the ceremony, calling me by name. I had never been in the presence of such important people before.

On our way back to the hotel, they let me sit up front in the jeep so I could take pictures. They warned me to be careful not to hold my camera too close to the window. African people don't like their pictures taken. Some have been put in prison for not asking before taking photos.

One soldier ran alongside the truck, forcing vehicles to move out of the way and keeping people from my door.

Our team met for supper at the hotel restaurant. One evening, back in my room, I turned the TV to their music video channel. Texting friends back home, I heard pop, pop, pop.

I left my room and walked onto the landing that led to metal stairs that wound to the alley below. I couldn't see anyone around.

I texted John, "Did you hear that sound?"

He messaged back. "I'll be down."

He met me at the end of the hall, and we looked around outside. We saw no one, and the sound had ceased.

Dismissing the sound, we returned to our rooms.

A little while later I heard it again. Pop, pop, pop!

"Are you hearing this? It sounds like gunfire." Through the curtains, I peered outside. In the middle of the street, a man glanced behind him and took off in a sprint.

"We hear it," John texted. "One of the guys is checking."

From my window, I saw the silhouette of a person squatting behind a large container at the corner. He appeared to be using his cell phone to video.

Ping.

"There is a shootout between drug dealers and the police," John messaged. "The hotel advised us to stay inside. We are safe. It doesn't involve us."

I sat on the bed and sent Mom a text, "Do you think this would be a good time to tell Dad that there is a gun shoot-out between the police and drug dealers in the street in front of our hotel? LOL!

"Probably not," she replied. Dad was not in favor of me taking this trip to Africa. I decided I would wait to tell him once I returned home safely.

"Well, God, that's all in your hands," I said as I pulled out M&M's and Coca Cola, and relaxed the rest of the evening with the sound of the gunfire in the background.

February 29, 2020. Day 16: The Unexpected

The director asked me to be his Assistant Manager of Translation Events in Africa. Today I started training to enter team projects, events, and workshops into the system and review the budget. I finally felt more like a part of the team.

Once we got to supper this evening, things changed. An achiness started in my neck and shoulders. Perhaps I had sat awkwardly, typing with my arms too high on the table all day. But the feeling worsened until I could hardly wait to finish the meal and stretch out in my room.

In my pajamas, I lay across the cool bedspread. Soon I felt feverish. At 1:00 a.m., I woke with chills and abdominal pain. At 4:30 a.m., I woke soaking wet with sweat.

I texted John early and told him I may be contagious with the fever. I slept nearly all day. For a while, I sat in the chair and looked out the window. "God, why bring me halfway around the world to have me sick and unable to be in the field?"

As soon as the guys returned, John knocked on my door. Despite the 90-degree heat, I wore my sweatshirt with my hood up.

"You look awful." John stepped inside while he spoke on the phone with his wife who was a nurse. John felt my forehead, and they went back and forth in their conversation, questioning me. John mumbled a word I didn't want to accept. Malaria. Still on the phone with his wife, John left the room.

I had all the symptoms; uncontrollable shaking chills, fever, aches, headache, abdominal pain, backache, faintness, and periods of profuse sweating.

That first night by the pool, the bites I received around my exposed ankle had carried the sickness into my bloodstream. Having stomach trouble, which was not unusual when I travel, I consumed a lot of antacids. I later learned antacids could cause the malaria medicine I had been prescribed to be ineffective.

Now I questioned God even more. "You promised me in the dream you would protect me from death and disease. Why have you allowed me to get sick?"

John initiated plans with the organization for an emergency medical evacuation back to the States. The next morning, the fevers and chills had stopped but the pain had worsened. I was too sick to go into the field with my team.

The decision was made that the President of the ECC would drive me to their local hospital. My blood pressure was 113/33. I thought for sure their monitor had to be wrong. They ran tests and took an X-ray of my abdomen.

A nurse led me to a chair in the doctor's office. "Sit down." The nurse motioned to the chair at the doctor's desk. The nurses didn't speak good English, and I was afraid I misunderstood. The doctor had paperwork spread across the workstation. I was afraid to sit at his desk, so I stood.

"Sit down there." The doctor with a little better English directed. I sat. Three nurses, two technicians, and the doctor gathered around. The doctor put the X-ray film on a lightboard that hung on the wall.

"I understand why you are in so much pain. You see this dark area?" He pointed at the massive black area in the film. "Your intestines are full. Too much constipation. There is no more room and it's backing up. The microbes have nowhere to go, so you are having fever and chills."

He gave me a prescription and told me in a day I'd feel better. As we checked out at the front counter, the ECC President asked, "What is wrong?"

"Constipation," replied the desk clerk.

This was not about constipation. That was the sickest I have ever been.

The following day, weak and headachy, I felt well enough to return to the school with the team and take part in the final day's celebration. When I arrived, the soldiers sitting outside the building smiled and stood, cheering, "Valer...oiu!"

They lined up to shake my hand. All day they came to me, praising God I was all right. I felt so loved by strangers. The director said the day I went to the hospital, the team of soldiers and facilitators spent a great amount of time singing and praying individually and corporately.

"I've never seen anything like it," he said.

On the trip back to the States, I felt pretty good considering what my body had just been through until the Monday after I returned home. Fever, headache, and chills resurfaced; typical of a malaria flare-up that cycles every 24-36 hours.

Our flight back was one of the few allowed to fly out due to the new Covid-19 virus that had filtered into Africa, and a few cases had just been found in the States. Some of our team flying home from other parts of Africa were stranded for weeks.

Covid-19 created another challenge. My headaches were horrendous, making it difficult to function. I scheduled an appointment to see my doctor who became fearful I had the Covid-19 virus they knew very little about yet. She fought with the Health Department over the phone about getting one of the few available swab tests. I qualified with my symptoms and had just traveled from another country. They told her my condition wasn't bad enough to warrant giving me one of the tests as their supplies were limited.

In the emergency room, a doctor with a foreign accent said, "Since you've been out of the country, and we don't know what this is, we need to admit you and keep you under observation by an infectious disease specialist." He added, "Don't go out of the country anymore. There is enough mission work here."

Though I agreed with him there is plenty of mission work in my own country, I found the comment frustrating. *I go where God calls me to go. Those people deserve to have the word of God, too.*

In the hospital, nurses and doctors came into my room gowned in yellow suits and masks. The news spread such a fear of Covid-19 family and friends were afraid to visit.

For three days, I was alone not knowing what I had, if I would live or die, and if I'd die alone. Some moments I knew I had God to walk me through. Other times, I felt disheartened and lonely as texts came in from family and friends saying they would not visit.

My prayers became questions. "God, help me understand. You told me in the dream I would not get sick. I've professed that as my testimony of faith. Why did I get sick? Can I not hear you? Did I not hear correctly?"

Then came the still small voice. "I told you I would protect you. I did not tell you, you wouldn't get sick."

I went back and reevaluated the dream in detail. When He told me in the dream not to worry because He would protect me, I was scared at that time of breathing in the death in the camp. He did keep His promise. I misunderstood what the promise entailed. He protected me from death when death knocked at my door.

For three weeks, I was sick. Three weeks to remain in peace and trust Him when I didn't understand.

With the Pandemic around the world, my test became my testimony.

CHAPTER THIRTY-TWO

Covid Cyclone

Journal

God, Covid?

Our doors have been forced closed. There are no sports, no church events, no festivals, schools are closed, businesses are closed. Everything my business is based around.

Today, my two remaining employees regretfully gave notice to leave for better-paying jobs with more hours. I can't compete. They need to support their families.

I feel failure, defeat, sadness, anger, relief, and excitement to see your plan. I don't understand why you want me to walk away, leave customers hanging, and stiff vendors out of what I owe them. I want every dime I owe paid off. They are trying to survive the pandemic as well.

Why would you not at least let me walk away with some integrity? I trust it will all work out, but I don't even know the next step to work toward. I don't know what is to come, but I want to find stability and rest soon.

I recall the words when the company was offered to me to purchase. "He says if anyone can turn this around, it will be you." They believed in me. And I stabilized sales for two years.

David Jeremiah said, "As you walk forward into your calling, you will be attacked every day."

Someone on the radio said, "He may be taking you through these trials today to give you strength for your tomorrow."

There are days I feel doom and gloom like this is all life will ever be. One trial, one hardship, over and over and where is hope?

There is something exciting about the thought you allowed this to prepare me to step into my call. Allowed it to build my strength to stand against what's to come.

In my dream the other night, the Holy Spirit spoke. "Faith doesn't come from getting what you want. Faith comes when you don't, and you trust him anyway."

Though my prayer wasn't answered to save my company, I continue having faith and trust you anyway.

The next morning, a printing company from out of town offered a lump sum for my client list, along with a job. They wanted me to stay six months to transition my clients to them. They told me to file bankruptcy to have a fresh start to go where God was leading and not look back.

I accepted the offer and accepted to trust God even when I didn't get my prayers answered the way I had hoped. I didn't want to close my business, but I was willing if this step freed me to do ministry work.

Grateful for the opportunity, I struggled with the idea of filing for bankruptcy. Everyone was suffering because of covid. I pleaded with God to allow me to pay every dime of my debt, then I promised to close the business and follow His call if that is what He wanted.

A friend had offered me a job before this other offer came about. I accepted the position. He allowed me to run my business rent and utility free in a corner of his office.

Within a month, life changed financially. God honored my request by allowing me to gradually pay down the debt while advancing in my new career.

CHAPTER THIRTY-THREE

Funnel Clouds Form

David was earning straight A's with his online education.

Maybe the attorney was right, and coming here was the best thing for David. He was staying out of trouble and doing well with his school work.

His release date was scheduled for one week after his school's graduation ceremony. We asked the attorney to request an early release for good behavior, so David could cross the same stage to graduate with his classmates. The prosecutor said it was too late for David to get his diploma. I believed with the power of prayer, God could do anything. And of course, his mom would be relentless about it.

With a letter, the judge honored my request and approved David's early release.

In the security check room, I waited excitedly for David to be brought from confinement.

A security guard walked into the room. "Are you David's mom?"

"Yes, I am."

"You've got a good kid there. I know he's gotten caught up in some trouble," he said. "But really, David's a great kid. You need to know that."

"Thank you for that." How refreshing to hear those words after all the negativity I received from the court.

On the day of his high school graduation ceremony, David crossed that stage with pride. With all the challenges we had faced to get here, saying I was a proud mother of what he had just accomplished was an understatement.

Once David settled in at home, I put some things away he brought home from the prison. In a folder was a letter from an inmate saying once the inmate was released in July, he would make David a partner in his business.

In my spirit, it was at that moment I knew our nightmare was not over. The worst was yet to come. The dreams were real; our enemy was not done with him yet.

On Saturday, I attended a funeral for the daughter of a special couple in our church. The lines were long, and it was difficult as I got closer to the mother. The tears welled and I couldn't choke them back.

Her tears had dried after hundreds had been past to hug her. She embraced me tight, and I felt like she supported me in that moment instead of the other way around. Her husband looked at me with compassion and kind eyes. We both cried as I choked out, "I'm so sorry."

Their daughter was David's age. They were in Sunday school and youth group together. They had both received their graduation Bibles from the pastor two Sundays before. The weekend prior, the family held her graduation party to celebrate her big accomplishments with goals of college and her future marked out.

Katie was a beautiful girl who brought joy to others. She accepted Christ in her life at a young age and lived out his love with her precious heart for others. People loved her and Katie loved people.

A car wreck took her life. A blocked stop sign and a restricted view at a cross-section and a beautiful soul was lost. One blink. It was difficult to watch Katie's family go through such devastation and loss.

The morning after the funeral, my phone rang.

"Well," Bob began, "the boys have been in a car accident. They were drinking. They crossed the center line, and the car was lodged on top of a boulder along the other side of the road when someone found them. They were both passed out. They're okay, but they are back in jail."

This was the call I feared I'd get one day.

David had only been home for a month. It was his eighteenth birthday, and the boys were invited to a big party in Fort Wayne. Both had been drinking, but when it was time to leave, Austin could barely stand.

In the car, Austin put the key in the ignition. David snatched the keys and refused to give them back. Austin got out to go around and take the keys from David. When Austin got out of the car, David jumped out and ran around to the driver's side.

David thought he could drive. They got on the road and then he blacked out.

Bob and I went to the autobody shop that held Austin's car for repairs. All I could do was stand there looking at the vehicle and praise God my two sons didn't lose their lives that night or take someone else's.

What really drove that point home, was that on the passenger's side, something had hit and shattered the side door window. The glass was caved in and formed, yet the glass was still intact. The realization hit hard, that God had chosen to protect Austin. Had the object been allowed to force itself through the shattered shards, it was positioned to travel in the path of where Austin's head lay sleeping.

I went to church that morning and sat in the back pew. When the worship team began the closing song, I walked to the front of the auditorium and asked the pastor if I could speak to the congregation.

He stepped aside and handed me a microphone.

"First, I want to thank you for the many prayers you have prayed for my boys over their use of drugs and alcohol," I said. "I came up here because I don't know what else to do. I am so tired of this fight, and I feel so alone. I just attended Katie's funeral here yesterday. This morning I received a phone call I was dreading I would get one day. Both of my boys had been drinking and were in a car accident."

I saw the pastor's wife grip the pew in front of her.

"I thank God they survived and didn't hurt anyone else. But I am questioning God as to why *my* sons are still alive? And I am thanking Him for second chances. Will you please continue to pray for them? I know David is saved, but recently, Austin told me he was uncertain what he believed. Please, pray God reaches them before it is too late, and pray for me to have the strength to get through this season. Thank you."

I handed the microphone to the pastor and started to walk away. He placed his hand gently on my back and said, "Let's pray for Valerie and her boys right now."

I wasn't sure if I had done the right thing. Some of the family who had just lost their daughter were there.

After service, the girl's aunt hugged me tight. "Thank God, for second chances." She said in my ear. "Yes, Lord, please give second chances, and another, and another. I am so sorry; we had no idea what you have been going through."

This was just the beginning.

CHAPTER THIRTY-FOUR

Drowning, Can't Breathe

As I turned into the hospital's entrance, I could see the flashing of the ambulance's red lights swirling their haunting glow across the dark parking lot.

It had been a long forty-five-minute drive to the ER. Did I make it in time?

David

I woke up alone that morning because the girl I love and I had a fight the night before.

I smoked a blunt, went to the kitchen to make food, and carried it to the recliner to watch TV in my bedroom.

I called one of my homies, and we drove around smoking weed and listening to thumping loud rap music. About 2:30 p.m., I had to go to work, so he drove to the factory across town where I had gotten hired. We were smoking our craftily rolled joints when we pulled in front of the building, the whole car hotboxed and smoky. Without a care in the world, I got out of the vehicle knowing I smelled like dank, my eyes were bloodshot, and I was high.

I went through the employee entrance and clocked in. I liked my job. All I did was put boxes in boxes, like the video game Tetris, and stick labels on the side.

I was doing my job and listening to music on my speaker when I noticed two dudes approaching from across the aisleway. During a previous shift, someone said I needed to stop smoking before work because they could smell it on me.

"You need to take a drug test, David," one of the guys said. "We have to talk to the lady at your temp service you went through and have her come do it."

"I won't pass." I didn't see the point in putting off the inevitable, so I grabbed my stuff, walked out, and called my homie to pick me up.

As I waited for him to arrive, the temp service lady called. "We can't help you find another job if you don't take the test."

I still needed a job. "All right, I'll wait."

What's crazy is I passed the test but got fired because I told them I wouldn't pass. I got in the car, and my homie and I left.

I just got fired from my job and my girl won't talk to me because she came home the night before and I was in my recliner nodding off from heroin. She yelled at me because she didn't want me on it. I denied it so she left. I told my bro to take me to get more heroin. What could I lose?

We went to the park, did a line, smoked weed, and then he took me home. My girl was coming by to get her stuff from my house in an hour, so I hit another line thinking I'd be good by the time she arrived. I had finished the burger my dad got for me and was sipping on a milkshake while playing on my phone, and that was the last thing I remember except darkness. Nothingness.

When I woke on my bedroom floor, people hovered over me. I couldn't breathe. I felt like I was choking.

Someone kept yelling, "Can you hear me?"

I can hear you. Why do you keep asking? But the words didn't come out.

They pulled me to my feet and walked me outside to the ambulance. Paramedics assisted me onto the stretcher where they strapped an oxygen mask on my face. I felt like I was suffocating.

At home, I was having a great phone conversation with Mark who was still in Texas. I heard a beep indicating someone was trying to call. Glancing at caller I.D., I saw Bob was the incoming call and let it go knowing I could reach him later.

He called again. And again.

"Hey, I've got to go," I told Mark. "Let me call you back." I hung up and dialed Bob.

"David just overdosed," Bob said. "The ambulance is here now."

"What happened?" I ran into my bedroom to change out of my pajamas and into clothes.

"I heard a noise coming from his room. At first, I thought he was coughing, but he was groaning. His door was locked, and he didn't answer when I knocked. I had to bust into his room and found him sprawled and unresponsive in his recliner. His eyes were rolled into the back of his head. I thought he was dead."

Dressed, I sprinted to the kitchen to get my keys.

"The cops had to use two narcan shots to revive him," Bob added. "It was some kind of narcotic."

In the garage, I jumped into the car. "I'm on my way!"

"I'll meet you there."

I couldn't press the garage door opener fast enough. As I turned onto the street, I asked aloud, "Is tonight the night, God? Is this the night you mean by losing my son?"

On the drive to the hospital, I recalled finding David two weeks ago in his room as he came down off meth. His mouth and lips were purple. Dark circles were around his bloodshot eyes. His skin was pale, and his blonde hair was an uncombed mess.

"David, you look horrible" I pleaded as I knelt beside his bed. "Will you please go to the hospital with me and get help?"

"I'm fine, Mom," he mumbled.

"You look like death warmed over," I countered. "You have to get help before something bad happens. Please! I'm scared to even leave you tonight."

"I'm just coming off meth." He stood and rummaged through his closet for a shirt. "I'm not going to do meth again. I don't like the way it makes me feel."

"David, meth isn't something you just quit on your own."

"Yes, I can," he insisted. "Please leave."

"I'm scared if I leave, I may not see you alive tomorrow."

"Nothing's going to happen." He gave me a hug.

I held him as long as he'd allow it. "I love you."

"I love you, too."

I walked out of his bedroom and closed the door behind me. Would that be the last hug and the last "I love you" I'd ever get?

Leaving his room, I passed portraits of the kids in the hallway. In the living room, Bob sat on the sofa. His eyes followed as I walked to the front door to leave. The look on his face reflected what I felt. How long before we would lose our youngest son?

In the driver's seat of my SUV, I sat in silence. I didn't want to leave. Staring at the front door, I wanted to run back inside and drag David to the hospital. But I knew until David was ready, it wouldn't make any difference.

That memory was vivid tonight as my headlights lit the road to the hospital. The previous episode had been bad. What would I see tonight? "God, is tonight the night that you mean?"

A sense of relief came over me as I pulled into the hospital drive, but simultaneously an anxiousness for not knowing what was next for us. The red lights revolved on the ambulance that had brought David to the ER. The flashing red glow cast a haunting

175

feeling almost like Satan laughing. He warned he wasn't done with my boys, and he wasn't done with me yet, either.

Once I was out of the car, a girl ran to me. As she drew closer, I recognized David's girlfriend.

She threw her long thin arms around my neck and sobbed into my shoulder. "I'm so scared!"

"I know." Longing to sprint inside, I knew at this moment she needed me to wrap my arms around her and comfort her as much as I needed God to do the same for me. I waited until she was ready, and we went in together.

At the check-in desk, I recognized a long-time friend of the family who meant a lot to me in my college days. "My son was brought here for an overdose," I quickly explained.

She nodded. "I'll let you know when you can go back. With covid restrictions, only one at a time and only family."

Bob let me go back first to see David. The nurse opened the sliding glass door and drew back the curtain ushering me in. There was my blond-haired, blue-eyed, handsome young son, with a bare chest, propped to sit up straight in the hospital bed. A respirator mask covered his nose and mouth, and his arms dangled loosely to his side with IVs penetrating his fair skin. A monitor beeped rhythmically. His eyes were closed, and his breathing was labored.

I gently took his hand. His eyes slowly opened, and a tear slid down his cheek. He tried to say something through the mask, but I couldn't understand the words. He closed his eyes again.

Is this the night, Lord, that I may lose my son?

> David
> When I got to the hospital, it didn't feel real.
> I saw my mom, but I didn't understand what she said. So many people were around me, nurses, doctors, and the cops. I'm lying there trying to calm down, and my mom is freaking out, and I don't understand why.

Watching David sleep, I noticed he would breathe and then stop. Breathe and stop. The reality hit that the respirator kept my boy alive. The nurse returned and I asked, "Isn't his chest supposed to be moving?"

"As long as his chest is moving up and down, he's fine." She checked the monitors and watched David intently. "I'm getting the doctor, and we'll get him another Narcan shot." She hurried from the room.

All I could do was watch, trusting God. In moments, the nurse came back with a syringe and inserted the needle into the IV tube.

"He will be here overnight," she said, "to monitor the fluid on his lungs."

I didn't want to leave but needed to let Bob know what just happened and give him a chance to be with David. In the lobby, I sat with David's girlfriend.

A little while later, it was my turn with David until the registration clerk said I had to leave. His room was ready on another floor and covid regulations didn't allow me to stay all night.

I kissed him on the forehead and followed the woman out of the room. She had been a customer of my mom's, and I had spent time at her house when I was going through tough days in college. She was a great encouragement for me back then.

"You're asking me to leave my son, not knowing if he will survive the night." I found it hard to remain kind.

"I'm really sorry," she said. "They'll bring him through here if you want to wait in the lobby for him to come through."

> David
>
> I felt fine at the moment, but then somebody said, "He's not getting enough oxygen" and I was out again. Back into darkness.
>
> This time felt like a bolt of lightning hit me when they gave me more Narcan. Then I was really coming to. The oxygen mask on me felt like I was in a wind tunnel. It was too much, and I tried to take it off, but they wouldn't let me except when I started to throw up.

I took a seat next to Bob waiting in the lobby. A dark-haired young man came in. When Bob greeted him, I realized he was one of David's friends. Sheepishly, he sat down and remained in silence. He had heard the news over the scanner.

I felt a moment of compassion for the boy and wanted to go over and hug him, but I didn't want to make it any more awkward for him.

When medical staff wheeled David through the atrium, we lined up like we were watching a parade, only this parade didn't bring smiles or joy.

The young man stared at David as he passed. Covered with white sheets and a light blue blanket, David tried to say something to him, but the words were muffled under his oxygen mask. Instead, he nodded at his friend.

They rolled the gurney through another set of large double doors, and he disappeared when the doors shut behind him. We stood awkwardly, not wanting to leave but knowing we couldn't stay.

Driving home I wondered. *Is he going to die tonight? Will I see my son alive again?*

In my journal, I wrote, "God warned me I would lose a son to drugs and alcohol. Tonight he extended grace. To what degree of loss did he mean I did not know. Satan warned me he wasn't done with my boys yet. So tonight I was having to face the question of what I will do if God's grace runs out and he uses my son's death as a testimony to reach others for Christ.

"Lord, hear my cry," I prayed aloud. "Have mercy on us. Please, don't take him from me. I pray he survives, and you turn him around. Your will be done; not mine. Just give me the strength to get through either way."

David

Things finally settled, and they took me to a different part of the building for the night. When they wheeled me to the other room, we went through the lobby and my homie was there. I tried to tell him I was good, but the mask wouldn't let me.

All I wanted was to see my girl, but they wouldn't let her in because of covid regulations. She left the hospital before they rolled my bed past the lobby where she had waited.

In my room, they switched the oxygen mask to tubes that went in my nose. What a relief. I finally got to call my girl. She was crying which made me cry because I felt bad for putting her through that. I was scared, and it was nice to hear her voice.

I tried to sleep after, which was hard because the fluid in my lungs made my chest hurt. They gave medicine for the pain. When I woke up the next day, my parents were in the room. My chest hurt, but the doctor said I should be fine and released me to go home.

CHAPTER THIRTY-FIVE

Shallow Breath

September 25, 2021

David

I had just served forty-five days in the county lockup because I had violated my house arrest for smoking weed and whizzing dirty every time. I was on the home detention bracelet that I wore around my ankle for possession of narcotics from the first time I overdosed. It was a long forty-five days because I was away from my girl, Ashlynn, and I missed her a lot. Phone calls with her always sucked because I loved to hear her voice, but I hated to hear her sad.

The day I was released from jail, she was there to pick me up. It's the best feeling in the world to just touch the person you love after not seeing them for a while. Felt like there was nothing else in this world, just us. It was like falling in love all over again.

I climbed into her car, and she drove me to my dad's house where I was going to be living. Once we got to the house, I called my probation officer to set up a meeting. That was the first step I needed to take once released.

"Call me back in a few days, David, and we'll get you scheduled."

"Okay, thanks!"

With that said, I decided to take advantage of that and drank for the next couple of days thinking I'd be good by the time I had to meet with her. I had already told myself and my girl I wouldn't smoke weed, and I didn't.

It's day three or four and even though I'm drinking, to me I was doing good because I wasn't using other drugs— until that night.

My brother Austin, his friend, and I all got together and started drinking. Ashlynn won't drink, so she stayed in my room while we were in my brother's bedroom. We were chillin' and having a good time when a text came across on my phone.

"You want some perc 30s?"

I was already drunk, so I was like, "F@#k it!"

I had to sneak out of the house to get them because I didn't want my girl to know.

"Are these real or fake?" I asked my supplier.

"They're real!"

I asked him three times because a lot of Perc 30s were being sold in our area laced with fentanyl and kids were dying. The pills came in either white or blue and these were blue, so I kept questioning him. I didn't want the fake ones with fentanyl. I just wanted the painkiller that would give me a high.

When I got back, I went in and checked on my girlfriend, and told her I'd roll up a blunt for her and the guys. I went back in the room and busted out the Perc 30s. I convinced Austin and his friend to do some, so I broke it into three pieces.

I crushed the pill and formed three straight lines of fine powder. Austin only did a small snort of the line, and I only did half of mine.

As I snuffed the powder and breathed it in, this feeling suddenly hit me and I thought, "Oh s$%t! Not again!" I told myself I was fine and ignored it.

Austin

Sitting on the bed, David, me, and one of our other friends were drinking and smoking together. Out of nowhere, David got a text asking if he wanted some Perc 30s. We weren't sure if it was going to be real or fake. Snorting the pain pill was supposed to give you a high and calmness. I decided that I wanted to try it after David did some persuading.

I only did a smidge because I was afraid that it really was fentanyl. I didn't do a whole line. David didn't do much either. I think my friend did a little bit more. After that, they decided to go out and smoke some weed in David's girlfriend's car, but I remained in my room resting on the bed texting my girlfriend.

David

We went outside to sit in my girl's car for a while. She climbed into the driver's side, I got in the passenger's side, and my friend got in the back seat. They were smoking the blunts I had rolled them, and we were chillin' listening to some rap music.

I reached down and was looking for something in my pocket; I always felt like I had lost something for some reason. As I rubbed my hand across my pant pocket, I felt the other pill. I forgot I had it! Going through my mind was, "I hope she doesn't reach over and feel it in my pocket." Then everything suddenly went black and I was out.

Ashlynn looked over and saw David with his head down, chin on his chest. At first, she thought he was just messing around.

"Are you okay, David?" She laughed, feeling high after inhaling the smoke from the blunt. "David?" After a moment of no response, she began to panic feeling something was wrong. "David, wake up!"

Austin

I was having a nice chat texting back and forth with my girlfriend when all of a sudden, my friend came running back inside the house, throwing my bedroom door open in a panic.

"David's not responding!"

At the same time, David's girlfriend ran in crying and screaming at Dad, "Call 911! Somethings wrong with David! He isn't responsive!"

I jumped up out of the bed and ran out across the yard to where Ashlynn now stood at the car. She was talking on the phone to someone.

"Who are you talking to?"

"The police," she answered.

As I looked in the car, she was right. David was motionless and didn't appear to be breathing! Still sitting in the front passenger seat of the car, he was limp with his head dropped forward and his eyes remained closed.

"David, wake up! Wake up!" I yelled as I grabbed a fist full of his T-shirt and shook him. I tried smacking his face, and there was still no response.

"I'm at 2017 Camden Court. My boyfriends not breathing."

"Okay." The dispatcher calmly responded.

"He's breathing, but he's not waking up."

"You say 2017 Camden Court, correct?"

"Camden Court," she repeated through tears. "Please hurry, please!"

"Okay. And what's your phone number?"

Ashlynn rapidly rattled off her cell phone number. "Please hurry!"

"How old is he?"

"Nineteen," she stated between her rapid breathing.

"And you can't tell if he's breathing or not?"

"He's trying to breathe, but he's not opening his eye lids, and he's like, 'Hhhh, Hhhh',"

she said as she tried to describe David gasping for air. "Oh, please hurry!" She begged while crying. "Please!"

"Do you know if he took anything?"

"He was drinking alcohol. Please hurry!" She frantically begged through her sobs.

"Okay... okay." The dispatcher tried to calm her. "Alright, take a deep breath for me. Listen. Listen."

"David, wake up!" Ashlynn continued to try to awaken him.

"Stay with me here. I need you to take a deep breath. We're going to... so he was drinking alcohol?"

"Yes!" she answered.

"Okay," the dispatcher said as she continued to gather information.

"Oh my God!" Ashlynn cried as she began feeling hopeless.

"I have a medical," the dispatcher stated as she spoke with the hospital on a second line. "It's at 2017 Camden Court, Huntington."

"Oh my God!" Ashlynn cried again in helplessness.

"We have a male that is not responding. He was drinking alcohol. She says he's trying to breathe, but he can't very well. She's upset— she's on the phone." Ashlynn began crying loudly in the background. "Ma'am. Ma'am."

"His lips are turning white!" she said with panic in her voice.

"His lips are white? Okay." The dispatcher continued as Ashlynn's sobs became squeals. "What's your name ma'am?"

"Ashlynn."

"Okay, I need you to take a deep breath. So we can help him, okay? I need you to talk to the hospital, okay?"

"Please, hurry! You have to hurry!"

"Ma'am, I need you to calm down," said the man from the hospital with sternness. "Listen to me. You need to calm down! Calm down so we can help him, okay? Are you with me?"

"Baby, baby! Baby, baby! They are coming, okay?" Ashlynn cried as she continued to talk to David.

"Calm down so we can help him," the man from the hospital again firmly stated with frustration in his tone.

"I'm sorry. Are you close?" Ashlynn whimpered.

"We are on the way. But I need you to calm down so we can help him!"

"I'm sorry. I'm sorry." She apologized as she tried to calm herself.

"How old is the patent?"

"He's nineteen." She began to breathe rapidly once more.

"Is he awake?"

"No, his eyes are closed. He's going, 'Hhhh, Hhhh'. He's not opening his eyes."

"Is he breathing?"

"Yes, he's trying. Barely. He's stopping." She softly began to whimper at a new realization. "He's slowing down."

"Alright, now listen to me," the man demanded.

"Sorry, sir." She apologized like a child being wrongfully punished.

"Now listen to me, okay?"

"I'm listening."

"I'm sending the paramedics to help you now. Stay on the line, and I'll tell you what to do next. Is he still unconscious?"

"Yes."

"If there is a defibrillator available, send someone to get it, and tell me when you have it."

She became quiet. "Oh, my God!" The sound of hopelessness was in her voice.

"Are you right by him now?"

"Yes."

"Listen carefully. Lay him flat on his back on the floor."

"Get him out of the car, Austin. Lay him flat on his back," she yelled frantically. "Get him out of the car."

Austin ran toward the car and tried pulling David out, but he was dead weight and he couldn't move him.

"And remove anything from under his head," continued the man from the hospital.

"Remove anything from under his head," she repeated coaching Austin.

"Get him flat."

Austin retreated. With the drug in his own system, he had no strength or ability to move David.

"He needs to be flat." Austin stepped away, giving up. "Austin, you have to get him out," she pleaded. With her phone still in hand, she tried to swing David's legs around and pull him out by the shoulders. David's dead weight caused him to fall and slump over the center console. She wasn't going to be able to move him either.

An excruciating pain penetrated Austin's heart as it dropped into the pit of his stomach. A feeling of loss and defeat came over him— had he lost his brother? His best friend! As tears streamed down his face and hopelessness overtook him, he threw up his hands and yelled, "This is why I didn't want to do it!"

"Do you have him flat on the floor?" asked the hospital.

"No!" She softly cried while out of breath from trying to move him.

The flashing blue and white police lights came around the corner. Austin ran to the house to get the remaining alcohol and drugs removed from their rooms.

"Oh, my God. They're here, can I hang up?" she asked.

"Who's there?" the man questioned.

"The cops... please." She paced frantically waiting for the police to exit their cars.

"Are they right there with the patient?"

"Yes," she answered and then began to speak to the officer who approached her. "Please get him out! We can't get him out!" On the phone, she continued, "They're here."

The officer inspected David. He was now pale, his lips were white, and he was not breathing. The two officers pulled him from the vehicle and laid him in the grass.

"We don't know what's wrong with him," Ashlynn explained. "He was drinking alcohol."

The officer asked what his name was and proceeded to tell the other officer that it appeared David had overdosed on something.

They administered Narcan through a nasal spray. EMTs arrived and tended to David's recovery. During a search by one of the officers, the plastic baggie with the remaining blue pill fell out of David's pants pocket. On one side of the pill it was marked with an "M"; the other side was marked "30".

Once David recovered from the Narcan, EMTs helped him to his feet. He looked with confusion over at Ashlynn who was standing in the driveway with her mom. The EMT's helped him into the ambulance and officers told Bob they'd be taking him to the hospital.

Evening had come after a long day at work, and my friend Tim and I had decided to hang

out at my house after supper, and then settled on the couch for a movie. Part way through, my cell phone rang. Bob was on the other end.

"Well, David overdosed again!" he said in a frantic voice. "Him and his girlfriend and another kid were all sitting out in her car drinking when she came running in screaming to call 911 that David was unresponsive. The cops showed up, and they had to use the Narcan on him again. They are on their way to the hospital. I can't leave. The cop wants me to stay here with Austin because he thinks maybe he took something too. He thinks he's not acting right, so I can't go!"

"Oh, geez! Okay, I'm on my way!" I said, as I was grabbing my purse off the kitchen counter. I had recently moved back to town where the kids lived, so I was only about fifteen minutes away from the hospital.

"My son David's here. A drug overdose." I choked out to the lady sitting behind the ER

counter. Once again, it was a dear friend of mine that I hadn't seen in awhile. I'm not sure why, but this time the emotions were higher, and I could barely get the words out. I felt a

sense of panic that I didn't experience the last time.

My friend began tapping the keyboard in front of her with eyes fixated on the computer monitor. She reached over and picked up the phone receiver punching buttons to call back to the ER department, "Do you have a David back there? An overdose. Mom's a little on the frantic side!"

Frantic! I thought. I've never been called frantic before. Maybe a little emotional or panicked, but frantic seemed to be such a strong word to describe calm and collected *me*.

"He isn't here yet. Please take a seat in the lobby area, and I'll let you know when he arrives and they are ready for you."

"Okay, thank you," I said as I turned to walk toward the all too familiar patterned loveseat across the hallway.

Tim had driven me to the hospital this time. He walked in the glass sliding doors about the time I got seated. We sat quietly waiting for the ambulance to arrive— and we waited— and we waited.

After a while, I was getting a little anxious. I walked up to the counter and asked, "Do you know why the ambulance hasn't arrived yet?"

"No, I'm not sure."

I sat back down and waited a little while longer. Still no ambulance.

I had been texting my parents and decided to call Bob. "Has the ambulance left yet? David isn't here."

"What do you mean he isn't there?" he questioned in surprise.

"I don't know. They say he isn't here. But the ambulance already left there, right?"

"Yes, they left with him about a half hour ago. The police came in and said they had him in the ambulance and they were getting ready to leave, but I needed to stay here with Austin."

"Okay, I'll let you know when he gets here."

Another fifteen minutes went by—

I approached the counter again. "Is everything okay? Why isn't the ambulance here with him by now?"

"I'm not sure. Maybe they had some trouble," she replied apologetically.

"What kind of trouble?" to which she couldn't respond.

I returned to the loveseat one more time, now with my mind running wild with thoughts as my leg nervously bounced. All I could picture was paramedics in their blue uniforms doing CPR on David in the ambulance and—

"God, is tonight the night? Is tonight the night you mean by losing my son?"

Bob called to ask if he had arrived yet, and I couldn't give him any explanation as to why they hadn't.

Another fifteen minutes…

"Can you check again, please?"

This time she went back to her computer to see what was logged.

"I'm sorry, but they don't even show him as being scheduled to arrive here."

"What do you mean it doesn't show him to be arriving here? He was in an ambulance on his way here."

"I'm sorry. I don't know," she said rather confused herself.

As I walked back to the dreaded chairs, I asked again, "God, did he die on the way? Is tonight the night, God? Is tonight the night you mean by 'I'll lose my son'?"

About that time, my phone rang. It was Bob. "He was seen at the annex?"

"The annex?" That was where they always took the boys for questioning. David's girlfriend had driven past the annex and saw David being walked into the building in handcuffs.

"You've got to be kidding me! The officers told you the ambulance was bringing him to the hospital, and no one came back to tell you he was okay and they weren't bringing him here?" I asked half in anger and half choking back the tears. "I've been sitting here waiting, thinking he died on the way!"

David

I woke up with a jolt when I got hit with the Narcan spray. The cops were all standing over me and I knew what had happened. All I could say was, "Are you taking me to jail?" I was worried because I felt for the pill, and it was no longer in my pant pocket, so I figured the police had confiscated it. I gazed around and saw my girl, her mom, and her uncle all huddled around me, and all I could feel was disappointment in myself. I continually asked, "Are you arresting me?" They just kept telling me, "Not at the moment."

They put me in the ambulance with its lights still illuminating the darkness of the night. They checked all my vitals to make sure I was stable and I seemed to be.

"Do you want to go to the hospital?" the EMT asked.

"No, I'm good."

"Okay."

They released me to the cops. "You need to come down to the annex with us to talk."

"Are you arresting me?"

"Not at the moment." And then they put me in the police car.

We drove downtown to the annex, which is where they perform their interrogations. They ushered me from the car into the building, leading me into a small narrow room with a single long wooden table and a few chairs.

"Why'd you do it?" demanded the officer.

"To get high," I responded.

"Did you know it had fentanyl in it?"

"Yes!" I told him.

"Why did you do it if you knew it could kill you?"

"Because I chase the high," I explained.

"Who'd you get it from?"

"I can't tell you that. I decided to do the drug on my own." There was no way I could reveal my source. That's a whole other danger in itself, and I wasn't going to be known for being a snitch.

"You're a piece of s$%t!" the officer barked when I wouldn't help them.

I sat there waiting for them to take me to jail after my questioning, but when the time came, they took me back home, which surprised me.

Being an addict, all I wanted was to get high or drunk, so that's what I did. I never did touch fentanyl or heroin again, though.

They put a warrant out for my arrest a couple of days later and picked me up three months later. I'm just glad it was me and not my brother who overdosed.

CHAPTER THIRTY-SIX

Undercurrent

Austin and I had plans to see a movie.

When I parked at the theater, he told me to wait a minute as he dialed his girlfriend on his speakerphone.

"Hi, are you there?" Austin asked when his girlfriend joined the call.

"Yeah," she replied meekly.

"Mom, I have something to tell you." He sounded nervous. "You're going to be a grandma."

"I'm going to be a grandma?" I said with surprise. "Seriously?"

"Yeah." He watched to see how I would respond.

I thought through my next words. Again, this wasn't the picture-perfect scenario for our family. They weren't married, and I had only met the girl a few weeks earlier. But I didn't want to make Austin feel condemned or take away from the joy of a child. And there was no changing the matter. Every child is a gift from God no matter the circumstances.

"Well, congratulations, Austin." I smiled. "You're going to be a great daddy."

"I have a praise," I announced the next weekend in Sunday school. "I'm going to be a grandma. Austin is having a baby."

Everyone quieted and the look on their faces showed their thoughts, but they were gracious enough to pray for him. After class, a friend walked with me to the sanctuary. She spoke about another mother who was over-enthusiastic and celebrating her unwed daughter being pregnant. In other words, I should not be making this situation out to be acceptable and right, especially to Austin; it was wrong in God's eyes.

I felt my frustration rising as she spoke, but I quietly listened to her view.

My boys had been raised in a Christian home. They knew what was right and what was wrong. They were old enough to make their own choices and live with the consequences. Who was I to condemn them? I, too, had made some poor choices, especially at that age. But conviction was the Holy Spirit's job. And I was pretty certain Satan would have his day with making them feel condemnation. It was my job as a mother to love him through it.

After what we went through with David's child, I found it harder to embrace this one as I did with Harper. I wanted to celebrate and let Austin experience the same joy as a married couple expecting their first child. So, I did what every excited grandmother did; we told close family, and I posted an announcement on social media for our friends and family to rejoice with me. Then began the planning.

Before long, I got the call there were complications, and they needed to deliver the baby at five months. The timing was far enough along to have a healthy baby, but I was concerned. The prayer chain began.

We had plans for Austin and me to be at the hospital that morning. He would be with her for the delivery. I waited anxiously in a small waiting room for my chance to hold this little bundle of joy and welcome her into our world.

Once she was born, Austin texted photos. When I saw pictures of this five-month-old preemie, I was flooded with anger, sadness, and heartbreak.

This can't be happening to us again. God, help us.

The photos showed a very healthy full-term baby. She and Austin had only dated for five months. There was no way this child was his. She had lied to Austin.

I telephoned Bob. "The baby isn't Austin's. We've got to tell him before he signs any paperwork. I need you with me to tell him."

I went to the nurses station. "I need some help, please." I showed the photos. "Is this a preemie baby or full-term?"

"The baby is full-term," a nurse replied.

"Can you get Austin, please? I need to talk with him. And," I requested with urgency, "don't let him sign anything."

I went back to the waiting room where three of his girlfriend's family members came in laughing, chatting, and carrying balloons and gifts. In contrast to their excitement, my excitement had deflated as quickly as if someone stuck a pin and burst a balloon.

Bob walked in behind them. I showed him the baby's picture. He shook his head in disbelief.

"You must be Austin's mom," her overly joyful mother approached.

"Yes I am." I grit my teeth in an attempt to hide my anger.

"Nice to meet you." She introduced, "I'm her mom."

I went back to the nurses station where an officer stood with a nurse.

"Is there any way we can have a private room?" I lowered my voice. "I really need to talk to Austin alone, and her family has just come into the waiting room."

The officer nodded. "I'll take care of it." He walked to the waiting room where Bob and her family remained.

I returned to the waiting area where Bob sat by himself. I hadn't seen the family leave the room, but I sighed with relief they were gone. A nurse led Austin to meet us and turned to go.

"Can you stay a moment, please." She looked surprised at my request but stayed.

Austin looked at his dad and me, waiting for something to happen.

"Austin, honey, I don't know how to tell you this, but that baby isn't yours." He looked confused, so I continued. "She told you the baby had to be delivered at five months right?"

"Yeah." He softly responded.

"That baby isn't a five-month baby, Austin. And since you've only been dating for five months, the baby cannot be yours."

The color drained from his face, and he looked like he was about to be sick.

"Austin, that is a full-term baby," the nurse affirmed. "I would not sign any papers."

God, how can this be happening to us again? That was the same look David had when I had to tell him. My momma's heart can't take much more of this. Why such terrible lies from these girls for both of my boys?

The next day, I met Austin at one of our favorite breadstick restaurants for lunch.

He slid his phone across the table to me. "Don't you think she looks like me, Mom?"

When he confronted her at the hospital, telling her he knew the baby wasn't his, her response was, "But how could that be? She looks just like you."

"There is just no way it is possible," I said. "I'm so sorry."

He stared at the picture. Later, he texted to say even if the baby wasn't his, he wanted to stay and help her raise the child. A month later, she told him who the baby's real father was, and he decided to leave the lies behind.

Both boys had lost the child they had come to love and the woman they loved. I had felt the loss of my first two grandchildren.

CHAPTER THIRTY-SEVEN

Breathe In

The pain was nearly unbearable with every click of the gun as sharp needles penetrated my skin over and over again like the staple gun of a carpenter.

I felt the technician wipe away small drops of blood from the fresh puncture wounds. My skin was hot with inflammation, and the area circled with the red marker felt like a hot iron had been laid across it. Now she started the second of three passes.

"Stop!" I cried, "Give me the gas. I thought I had a high pain tolerance, but I can't stand it any longer."

She set the ablation gun in its cradle and left the room to get the happy gas machine.

My leg was red and stung like fire. This pain I could handle, but the needles puncturing the skin at a deeper level took my breath and brought tears to my eyes.

She returned, rolling the cart containing the two tanks. *I can't believe I'm such a wimp.* When I had a C-section, the nurse said I hadn't used much of the morphine drip. "You can push that bottom as much as you need to."

"No, I'm good," I proclaimed.

"You must have a high pain tolerance," she observed. "You haven't used much."

Where was my high tolerance now? This was a minor procedure compared to a C-section.

"People really do this without the gas," I asked the tech.

"Some," she said. "I had a lady yesterday do it. A lot of people think they have a higher tolerance than they actually do."

She placed the T-shaped plastic piece in my mouth connected to the silver tank that held the gas meant to help me relax.

My head quickly felt fuzzy, my arms relaxed, and the roar of the machine kicked on. Click, click, click. She resumed puncturing the skin on my leg.

"Oh, my gosh! I still feel the needles breaking the skin with every click." The numbing gel she applied and let set for forty-five minutes under the saran wrap didn't work. My thigh was not numb. I would have to endure this for another two passes and the second leg.

Breathe in, Valerie. The more you breathe, the less intense you feel the pain.

Though I was under the gas and my mind felt hazy, something became clear. This is what it is like for those using drugs. They are trying to mask their pain. This must be what it is like for my boys. The more they inhale or consume, the less pain they feel.

I now had the answer to what many have questioned. *Why do people do drugs and alcohol?*

Breathe in, Valerie. Just like I needed to ease the pain and suffering when there was nothing else to numb it, that's what my sons and their friends were doing. Attempting to numb life a little. As I tried not to focus on the pain being administered to my flesh, I realized something else. I had a message to tell them.

"Instead of the drugs and alcohol, breathe in Jesus. The more you breathe him in, the less pain you feel," I wanted to say. "That doesn't mean the pain isn't there, but with Jesus, we can bear it much more just like this gas took the edge off my punctured flesh."

"Breathe," I mumbled aloud when the tube was removed from my mouth. "Breathe in more of Jesus."

"What?" The tech leaned in to hear.

"People use drugs and alcohol to numb their pain," I said. "Tell them to breathe in more of Jesus. The more you breathe him in, the more of the pain they can handle."

"That is so true." The tech went back to finish her work.

A cloth that contained a cooling gel was applied to my wounded skin. The soothing comfort made me think of the embrace of God when I'm going through hardship or sadness.

Breathe in. Breathe in more of Jesus.

CHAPTER THIRTY-EIGHT

Washed White

With a broken heart, Austin began drinking more. The mother of the young man who was involved the night they all went car hopping and who stole one of the guns, took revenge on Austin. She had her son set up plans with Austin, asking him to pick up some alcohol and meet him at the park.

Austin did as his friend asked, not knowing it was a trap. The kid's mother was sitting nearby in a dark alley and called police. He never made it to the park. They picked him up at a gas station nearby and he was once again charged with possession. Back to jail he went.

I lost my home, I had lost my business from what it once had been, I had lost my first two grandchildren. Now I lost my boys to a season of incarceration because of drugs and alcohol.

You were right, Lord. It is as you had said it would be.

Austin had been in jail a little more than a month when the option of a rehab program was discussed. I called an officer who I knew was a Christian and asked if he could recommend a faith-based rehab program Austin could apply for.

Austin applied to Inspiration Ministries and was accepted into a nine-month residential rehab program. My hope was restored; results came that I never expected.

Earlier, Austin told me he didn't know what he believed, so I felt equally surprised and grateful he was willing to enter a Christian program. During his time at Inspiration Ministries, I saw changes I had hoped I would one day see in him.

As I sat on the couch one evening, my phone rang, "Mom, I need to tell you something," I waited in anticipation. "I gave my heart to Jesus!"

Tears welled up and ran down my cheeks; this time, they were tears of joy. My prayers had been answered.

With a grateful heart and hands held high I praised God for goodness, "Thank you, Jesus! Thank you!"

The night of his Celebrate Recovery graduation, one of his house mentors stood and spoke highly of Austin, sharing that even at work Austin walked as a man of God. Generally quiet, Austin had asked this mentor to meet with him and read a book of the Bible together. Leaders commented Austin was one of the rare guys who took notes during services.

That night, shy Austin stood in front of a room full of people who showed their support by beating on the tables as they whooped and hollered for him. He read a beautifully written exit letter. In his closing statement, he read, "This program, and most importantly the good Lord, saved me from prison and myself. Jesus answered my prayers and restored my family relationships. I will never forget this time of my life and the love shown by you all. God bless!"

While at Inspiration Ministries, Austin was baptized in front of a small group of housemates. The following year, Austin and his girlfriend were baptized at the church our family attended. In a video played on the screens in the sanctuary, Austin shared his inspiring testimony.

1 Thessalonians 5:17 (ESV) tells us, "Pray without ceasing." I never stopped praying for my son. This mother's prayer was answered. Austin was breathing in more of Jesus. God was moving in his life.

David had given his life to Christ in an unusual way at a young age. One evening their stepdad was gone for the night, and the boys and I decided to camp out in the living room for some quality time together and a little fun. As I stood at the TV preparing the DVD to watch the movie *Passion of the Christ*, David struck up a conversation about his stepdad.

"Why does he say bad words?" David inquired. "When you are a Christian, you aren't supposed to say bad words. Isn't he a Christian, Mom?"

"Yes, he is. We are all at a different place in our walk though. No one is perfect. Some people are like baby Christians, and then they mature in their relationship with the Lord. God helps them to grow and change for the better over time." I explained. "It doesn't make him a bad person. But that's why it's important to accept Christ into our lives and be ready if God should decide to return."

"Yeah, I did that!" He proclaimed.

"You did what?" I asked with curiosity.

"I asked Jesus into my heart."

I turned and faced him in surprise. "When did you do that?"

"When I was five. Almost six." David had just turned six a couple of months before.

"Where were you? Were you at church?"

"No, I was in my bedroom."

"Was someone with you?" Now I was really intrigued.

"No. I was alone."

"Did you hear a preacher on tv or something?" I couldn't fathom how or who led my six-year-old to this big of a decision.

"No, I was just sitting on my bed one day and something told me to do it!" He said in his sweet little boy matter-of-fact way.

I couldn't believe my ears. "That was the Holy Spirit, Davie! God must have big plans for you someday."

Chills went through me. I had never in all my life heard of a child being alone in his room and being led by the Holy Spirit to accept God into his life, without someone there to influence or lead them. I knew then and I know now, God was going to use David in a big way someone day.

There were many times through David's years of growing up, that I saw an amazing gift of wisdom in him. Things he just knew that he had never been taught in the natural. As a young boy, he would lead many of his friends to come to know Christ as their savior.

David and I had many conversations about his faith and his prayers, while he was incarcerated. Satan made it clear that he wasn't done with my sons. But God wasn't done with them yet either.

It was David who first gave me permission to share our story; his story. "Go ahead, mom! If it's going to help people, do it!" He said over the phone from the jail one night.

David was maturing and went on to a rehab striving to get the help he needed to overcome his addictions. Both boys are following their dreams in careers fitting for them.

My hope in Christ who strengthens me has multiplied.

CHAPTER THIRTY-NINE

When Storms Break

"I don't know how you got through it all," is the comment I often hear from those who know my story.

Through another dream, I was given the words, *If unseen by a warrior.* At first, I thought this was the title of the book I was to write. When I questioned God about what those words meant, He helped me understand faith is something unseen. A warrior is one who continues to have faith even when they can't see God. When I go through trials and tests in life, I am to remain faithful to him, to trust Him, and to keep fighting against the enemy.

I learned many lessons through these storms, but one thing for certain is Satan and his demons are real. They sneak in slyly, and you don't realize what is happening until you are caught up in the fray. He is a liar, but sometimes a lie is easy to recognize. His use of half-truths is a weapon with great power to deceive.

Evil walks among us trying to destroy our families, our emotions, and our homes. He wants to steal joy and keep us defeated. We can choose to be defeated and stay defeated, or get back up, lift our swords, and fight the enemy with the power God gives. Just take His hand. God's word has power.

I learned when I felt I couldn't get out of bed from the weight of the trials I was going through, God will carry me through. I just have to ask Him.

When I began to have spiritual dreams, I realized they had one thing in common. No matter the battle or evil that was present, the dream always ended with me crying out to Jesus. Sometimes, speaking the name Jesus is the only word I can say while going through challenges larger than my abilities to handle. I promise He hears and sees us.

I believe God showed me the truth of the power in the name of Jesus through the dreams so that I would understand the answer through my trials. *Our* trials. When we walk through the storm, the answer *is* to call upon Him.

When the demon came to me in my sleep and told me, "I have your boys. I'm not finished with them yet, and I'm not done with you yet either," I felt terrified for days. For the next twenty-four hours, I could feel the demon's finger pushing on my arm.

One day, I walked past my TV listening to Beth Moore teach, and in passing, I heard her say, "Satan may not be done with you yet, but neither is your King." What freedom that statement gave to me. I felt fear lift, replaced with reassurance God was on my side and going to battle *with* me.

In trials and seasons of tests, we choose how to react to adversity. Joyce Meyer shared her husband enjoyed playing golf. She asked if he could never play golf again, what would he do?

"I'll be all right," he said, "because I've already thought about that and *decided* I'll be okay."

When I heard the Holy Spirit say if I followed his calling, I may lose my dream home, my business, and one of my sons to drugs and alcohol, I had no idea what that meant. What did *lose* mean? To what extent?

But God is gracious.

The bank could have taken my home from me, but instead, the Lord prepared my heart and led me to sell before that could happen. I lost the house, but it wasn't taken from me.

The business was at the point of bankruptcy. He could have made me file and close the doors for good. Instead, He honored my prayer and provided a way for me to downsize and pay off all my vendors. As I promised, I let the business go and stepped into this calling. He led me into ministry work and a new career that I enjoy.

He could have let my son die when David overdosed. Both boys could have died in the car wreck. Instead, He spared their lives. I only had to lose them for a season to the world of drugs, alcohol, and imprisonment. Before I knew what *lose* would mean, I had to *decide* no matter what, I would trust God and I'd be okay.

People have asked, "How were you able to say yes when God said you may have to lose your son? I don't think I could do that."

A valid question and I pondered the answer for a while. Did I want to give up my dearly beloved son? Absolutely not! Did God want to give up His son?

I had seen God work in my life enough to know if He asked me to give up my treasured child, there had to be a reason. He would use this for His glory. He would give me the strength to get through.

God prepares, God provides, God protects, and God can help me persevere. When the outcome isn't as I expect, God is always good.

This season of life was ugly and evil. With all that had happened, I felt worthless and empty. I was weary from the pounding of the wind of dangerous storms. I didn't have the chance to catch my breath before the next wave hit. Then the sea became calm. Life became more peaceful, and God did something I didn't expect. He put a friend in my life to walk beside me for a period of restoration and to remind me through his tenderness and his love, how God viewed me through his eyes.

To him, I was this beautiful and beloved princess. Sometimes I needed to be reminded despite the chaos I will have to live through in this fallen world, there is a God who sees me as valuable, as special, and I am loved by Him in measures I cannot grasp. He is a gracious and loving Father.

I learned no matter how women are treated; we are princesses in God's eyes. He is our husband when we need that void filled. God became mine for a period, and it was a beautiful time of my life spent with Him. He cares about our hearts more than we do.

A week before my first speaking engagement, I prayed for truth and closure about David's baby. For five years, I carried the pain of not knowing what happened to Baby Harper.

I felt nudged to reach out to the girl. No matter what the truth was, I couldn't let the enemy keep hold of my heart any longer. I needed to forgive her so bitterness no longer reigned in my heart, and I wanted to possibly free her from any guilt she may have felt in correlation with our family.

Hoping her phone number was the same, I sent a message. "I want you to know I forgive you."

I didn't expect a response, but a day later, she wrote back. "When you sent a text out of the blue, I felt it was God helping me to heal."

She had carried guilt for five years, affecting her life so much a few weeks earlier she began therapy. In a phone conversation, she admitted she did abort the baby. The words were painful, but with them came the release of knowing the truth. I could rest and have peace. Satan could no longer use lies, and I can celebrate my granddaughter, Baby Harper, who's in the care of my Jesus.

Abortion doesn't just affect the woman but affects the father, siblings, grandparents, and many more similar to the ripple caused when a rock is thrown into a lake.

And then God.

Our God is good and gracious. On the cross, Jesus took the penalty for all our sins and forgave us before we knew Him. We merely accept His gift.

If you struggle with addiction, anger, guilt, or anything else, you may feel God could never forgive you, that you've done too much wrong, that you are not a good enough person. Please, don't listen to those lies. God granted forgiveness on the cross. He offers a relationship with Him to anyone who accepts His son, Jesus, as Lord and Savior of their life.

If you want that relationship right now, don't wait! To help, here is a prayer you can say and accept Jesus into your heart right now!

Thank you, Father God, for your unconditional and unfailing love. Thank you for forgiving me when I have missed the mark and sinned. Please be Lord and Savior of my life. In Jesus' name, Amen.

Welcome to the eternal family of the God who created you. I encourage you to find a local church where you can connect and belong and grow in your faith with a community of others who are also growing in their faith. A place He calls us to gather to encourage and be encouraged. Together we can do more to advance His kingdom.

CHAPTER FORTY

Hope

Whalf about the rest of my story?

If you are going through a similar experience with your teenagers' using drugs and alcohol, I want you to know I share our story so you know someone else understands. You are not alone. I felt like I had no one to turn to. God gave discernment, wisdom, strength, and courage to get through. Ask him to help you. I promise He hears you. Reach up and take His hand.

When I returned from Africa, I didn't understand why God took me halfway around the world. Initially, I thought the journey was to become the director's assistant as he requested, and I accepted. Once covid hit, trips to Africa halted, and some had to find other jobs, including the director. My position was no longer needed.

One day, a young man named Wisdom called and asked for an appointment with me to do his taxes. He insisted I meet with him that day before he left the state for another job. When he entered my office, I discovered he was from Nigeria. As I gathered his data, he noticed the photos I had taken that hung on my wall of two African children playing and fishermen on the Nile River in Congo.

He pointed to the pictures. "Is that Africa?"

"Yes, it is." I told him about my trip, how I wanted to meet the teachers and children but didn't get to, and how I planned to write a book and speak.

One year later, I received a message from Wisdom wanting to know if I would speak at his company's Educational Summit in Nigeria. What began as encouraging and nurturing two hundred middle and high school teachers has grown into touching the lives of thousands. I didn't get to meet the teachers and children while I was in Congo, but God knew my heart and allowed me an international ministry that reaches into Africa.

We never know where God will take us if we are willing to follow.

God Prepares

God Provides

God Protects

God can help us Persevere

And God can Restore.

EPILOGUE

He gently took my hand and led me to a chair in front of the brightly lit Christmas tree at my parents' home.

The gentleman that he is, he got down on one knee. "Our paths have crossed many times in the last twenty-plus years. You know you are very special to me. You are my princess and"—he pulled a little black box from his vest pocket. Inside was a gorgeous, sparkling diamond ring. "I'd like to be your king."

"Maybe," I softly replied. The room grew quiet, and my family waited. His face wilted.

Why would I not accept? God allowed our paths to cross over and over for more than two decades. The first time I met him was when he passed by as I visited his wife in their living room.

"Hello," he greeted cordially.

First, we were acquaintances, then we served together on the board of my non-profit. He became my accountant, a dear friend, and then my boss during covid.

When his wife sadly passed away, my heart was tender for my dear friend. I wanted to make him smile and hear his laugh again. The spark had died from this jolly man. I wanted to celebrate her, go wherever he wanted to go, and help him experience joy and life.

And so, we did. We had been nearly inseparable for three years. We traveled, became business partners in three ventures, bought a lake house retreat, and started our journey in ministry.

We both had shattered hearts. God set us on this path of helping each other heal. It began as two friends there to help one another whenever we could. Early on, he knew there was more to come in our relationship. For me, it took much longer.

Eventually, I realized I miss him when he's gone, I don't want to do life without him, and the little seed of love God planted for my dear friend grew roots. He was my best friend and who better to marry?

I never in my wildest dreams imagined I'd one day marry Timothy D. Armstrong, but I know the kind of husband he was to Barb, and I always admired them from afar. If I can only have half of what they shared with one another, my heart will be forever full.

Tim is one of the most gentle, compassionate, caring, and loving men I've ever met.

With my family around me that Christmas, and this man on one knee, offering a ring and a life together, I said, "Yes! It's a yes!"

And then we said, "I do!

The end can sometimes be just the beginning.

V ALERIE JUILLERAT, is the founder of Lessons of the Heart Ministries, an international ministry seeking to bring healing, hope and encouragement to the hurting through a global outreach including podcast, television, the Internet, live events and books. She is an international speaker, artist, and author. She has been published in the books, *Anchor in the Storm* and *Refreshed by His Mercy*. Valerie carries a Bachelor of Arts degree in graphic design and is also a tax professional.

Valerie speaks at churches and venues sharing her testimony through a multi-media presentation, *"Finding Hope When Storms Don't Cease"*, sharing where she found hope through the loss of her business, her home and her sons to the world of drugs and alcohol. She has been featured on Wisdom Word Tv Christian Broadcast Network, Chandelle TV+ and at Chandelle Global Education's Teacher Summits speaking to thousands of African teachers. Valerie and her husband Tim, live in Fort Wayne, Indiana.

URGENT PLEA!

Thank You For Reading My Book!

*I really appreciate all of your feedback and
I love hearing what you have to say.*

*I need your input to make the next version of this
book and my future books better.*

*Please take two minutes now to leave a helpful review on
Amazon letting me know what you thought of the book.*

Thank you so much!

Valerie Juillerat

BOOK VALERIE FOR YOUR

FINDING HOPE WHEN STORMS DON'T CEASE
PRESENTATION

LESSONS OF THE *Heart*
by Valerie Juillerat

LESSONS OF THE HEART MINISTRIES

A Multimedia Presentation
consisting of drama, film, music and speech
that will give hope through the storms of life,
demonstrate God's provision, mercy and grace,
and challenge one's faith to a deeper level.

VISIT:
VALERIEJUILLERAT.COM

" *This event was phenomenal!!!*
It was so encouraging to see how Valerie stayed
strong in the Lord while weathering her storms. I
would definitely recommend seeing this if you ever
get a chance to. Amazing story of faith, hope and
strength."
M. Bigelow

" *I'm so glad I was able to attend this. Your story is*
very compelling, heart wrenching and powerful!"
L. Griffith